TRIPTYCH

The Three-Legged World

Peter Grandbois

In Time

James McCorkle

Orpheus & Echo

Robert Miltner

TRIPTYCH

The Three-Legged World

Peter Grandbois

In Time

James McCorkle

Orpheus & Echo

Robert Miltner

Etruscan Press

Etruscan Press
Wilkes University
84 West South Street
Wilkes-Barre, PA 18766
(570) 408-4546

www.etruscanpress.org

Published 2020 by Etruscan Press
Printed in the United States of America
Cover image: *Failed Monuments*, 2014 © Garry Noland
Photograph courtesy of EG Schempf
Cover design by Carey Schwartzburt
Interior design and typesetting by Aaron Petrovich
The text of this book is set in Williams Caslon Text.

First Edition

17 18 19 20 5 4 3 2 1
Library of Congress Cataloging-in-Publication Data

Names: Grandbois, Peter. Poems. Selections. | McCorkle, James. Poems. Selections. | Miltner, Robert. Poems. Selections.
Title: Triptych / Peter Grandbois, James McCorkle, and Robert Miltner.
Other titles: Three-legged world. | In time. | Orpheus & Echo.
Description: First edition. | Wilkes-Barre, PA : Etruscan Press, Wilkes University, 2019.
Identifiers: LCCN 2018015479 | ISBN 9780999753422 (paperback)
Subjects: LCSH: American poetry--21st century.
Classification: LCC PS617 .T75 2019 | DDC 811/.608--dc23
LC record available at https://lccn.loc.gov/2018015479

Please turn to the back of this book for a list of the sustaining funders of Etruscan Press.

This book is printed on recycled, acid-free paper.

Poetry's roots lie in the communal. The first *sceops*, or shapers of words, recited their poems to an audience gathered about the fire, and later the mead hall, one poet beginning where the previous ended. Only recently has poetry shifted to an isolated activity written by a solitary writer and read by a lone reader. *Hwaet!* The communal origins of poetry have returned in *Triptych!* What a great joy to share this space with two poets whose mythological hauntings and metaphysical—musings dance so tantalizingly with my own. Buy a book. Take a seat, and welcome back to the hearth!

—Peter Grandbois

In these three distinct, discrete, and demanding collections within a single cover, what connects them all is the attention to the celebrant's voice. If poetry is anything it is the pleasure of the poet in their language—whatever the poem may mean is ancillary to the velocities of language, the inhabitations that language creates, formal or densely scattering, historical or local. Each of these collections offer readers a dwelling in language, the extension of voice across poems and into poetry-making / *poiesis* / formations. These are individual formations and velocities, yet as the collections become proximate, they are near to each other, sharing the pleasures of this work, this in/forming.

—James McCorkle

The poets in *Triptych* are experimenting with poetry's innovative possibilities and unexpected potential. Peter Grandbois' *The Three-Legged World* offers lyric meditations on stance, speech, and sonority. James McCorkle's *In Time* computer code-like lines explore the relationship between breath and line breaks. Robert Miltner's *Orpheus & Echo* evokes fragments of lost texts that straddle the intimate distance between the prosaic and the poetic. Reading *Triptych*, a unique three-books-in-one collection, is like attending a seminar on twenty-first century poetics.

—Robert Miltner

Foreword

One Blue Boat   Three Triangulated Islands

Authorship can be tricky. Intimate and personal, it forges a contract between utterance and sign. It is the signature of purpose. It gives heartbeat a page count. Yet, authorship is vagrant and provisional. It disdains age, change of heart, or death. Authorship can be paradoxical, as in Anonymous; fraught, as in the Bible; faked, as in Ossian; or contested, as in Shakespeare. Maybe authorship isn't a real ship at all, only a Homeric clash of arms. Yet, there is the codex with all appurtenances: title, blurbs, launch, reviews, and sequels. Post-Gutenberg, the singular mark of authorship is the book.

Triptych disrupts conventions of book authorship. Between two covers are three books.

The Three-Legged World is a book by Peter Grandbois.

In Time is a book by James McCorkle.

Orpheus & Echo is a book by Robert Miltner.

They are nonconsubstantial. They are bound by no prior agreement or collaboration. There is no aesthetic reason for the order (alphabetical by…wait for it…author!). *Triptych* is not the product of a contest, program, solicitation, or advertisement; it has no precedent with this publisher. *Triptych* is not a means to package verse. It is not a selection or sampler. It is not a special issue. Peter Grandbois and James McCorkle are veteran Etruscans, and Robert Miltner is a valued colleague; but these authors had not colluded, discussed, or even met. Their books crossed the transom independently from diverse parts.

Of course, books converse with other books, and poetry, rippling from unmeasured sound into rampant forms, is especially polyphonic. Etruscan brings these three books together because they exerted upon our editors a gravitational pull, causing the shadow of one to fall across the reading of another. Sufficient on their own, these books achieve new altitudes when aligned.

When Grandbois, McCorkle, and Miltner were invited to read each other's books, they sensed the congruence, and embraced the venture enthusiastically. In fact, without conspiring toward a collaboration which was not conceived, each poet seemed to have augured the triad.

Grandbois: Everything is the source rising in the water/Column rising only to rise/ Into relation to others

McCorkle: The secret to the world lies at the borders.

Miltner: One Blue Boat   Three Triangulated Islands

Triptych launches no school. It backs no cause. What these books share is not easily labeled. None follows narrative conventions. None dwells on confession. None abides predictable meter. None is easily parsed.

Each climbs eerie heights where ego finds no purchase. Each takes a kaleidoscopic view of selfhood.

Each takes flight toward apotheosis. Each blesses the moments "Before we turn into air," or give way to "tongue of trees, language of clouds," and before "Gods and dogs begin their talking back," before birds "are falling through their late bodies." In Miltner's ogham-deep caesuras, in McCorkle's speech-song, and in Grandbois's cadences which whisper like ghostly passersby, "sound is emanation," and emanation asks, "what would this line be without the words?"

Or, what would a book be without books? 64 pages of loneliness? An unstarred Goodread? A spine stranded beyond the top rung of the library ladder?

So, *Triptych,* where authorship spirals into othership.

The world changes
As the leaves shiver from green to silver
In the wind, nothing owned.

Etruscan Press, June 2018

Table of Contents

THE THREE-LEGGED WORLD
Peter Grandbois

IN TIME
James McCorkle

ORPHEUS & ECHO
Robert Miltner

TRIPTYCH

The Three-Legged World

Peter Grandbois

In Time

James McCorkle

Orpheus & Echo

Robert Miltner

THE THREE-LEGGED WORLD

Peter Grandbois

Para Fernando, and Álvaro, and Alberto, and Ricardo, and . . .

"I know the world exists, but I don't know if I do."
--Fernando Pessoa

I

There is no one to write this

I wake and I am   an un-knowing,

two people at once   each un-reconciled.

Will I un-done be   swallowed by mad song

fearful of birds and   the way they shake fire

off their wings at dawn?   Or, un-stitched by rain,

will I bloom to sky   like a trout leaping

through un-bidden air?   Will I un-thought

dissolve into ground   a derelict holding

in his fat belly   hunkering down

until un-sought by   medusa night?

Or, un-handed by   my life's splintered wood,

is it possible   to float far above

this axe-hacked weather?   It's un-clear what skin

binds us to this darkened   field and why only

with an un-lit candle   can we even dream

of walking across.

[Sometimes when I wake]

Sometimes when I wake
to this whispering of leaves

I want to ask—*who are you?*

And by that I mean
this person in my bed

twitching like an epileptic
through another fever sleep.

If only I could escape this tunnel
in which so many selves are buried,

like a stunned ant climbing out
of a cave in,

fighting each grain of sand
to make its way back

to the broken neck of the world.

[Sometimes I think I hear]

Sometimes I think I hear my voice rummaging around in the next room, shouting about this insignificant map of the world.

It doesn't like being alone. The way memories grow thick as trees. Regrets rooting around you.

Once it played a trick and called to me in the voice of one I'd loved. But I saw the trap's teeth jutting through the pine needles across the bedroom floor. We know each other too well.

Lately, it's started taking credit for little things I do. Getting the groceries. Doing laundry. That sort of thing. It's relentless. I would tell it to shut up if I could.

I would say, "This poem is mine. This poem is more real than you."

I would say, "It's okay that we've parted company."

We do not come here to remain whole.

All that can be heard

Sometimes I am almost dead

Nothing but a sound of voices
Turning in the dark,

Or is it the darkness speaking,
And I am the nothing,

The child inside
Another word for stillness,

For a wilderness of rain
In which to bathe,

As if we didn't want
To take our names with us,

As if one voice alone
Could be heard,

When the day drains away

And all that's left is to listen
To the thrill of stars

That fall like bees in the night.

I'm talking to you. Can you hear me?

Take the ghost from your ears
And wait until silence

Is a book without end,
A moth-eaten world gone mute,

Until you are the silence.

I am talking
to you. I am

Talking to you.

[Sometimes when I look at myself I see]

Sometimes when I look at myself

           I see nothing

but inconvenient limbs,

         a river of spare parts.

Those days, I'm like a traveler

           who finds himself

in a strange town

         where even the trees

hold their breath

          knowing only the cold

is real.

         If this sounds

like the opening

          to a bad movie

or a new you,

        remember one tree

does not make a woods,

            and it's difficult to judge

the depth

         of even the smallest

river.

There are no secret lives

You cannot hide in water
or fish will make a home
of your bones, a refuge
within the spaces between
your ribs. You cannot hide
in air as the weight alone
is impossible to bear.
Forget about earth. It's
the first place they'll look.
Which leaves only fire, and
you'd have to be a saint
or an idiot to hide there.

Don't think for a moment
that eyes won't swarm you
like a river of bees,
that mouths like black widows
won't crawl around the back
of your neck then between
your lips. Don't imagine
that any of this is as real
as what you'll do to yourself
if you can only remember
in what room, what closet,
what time-darkened drawer
you've stolen yourself away.

As if darkness doesn't come drop by drop

I never feel

    where I am

but where my darkness

    pretends to be.

The ring of crickets

    beneath my feet,

the door to shifting

    floors on which I crawl

backward and blind,

    as if I've become

some thing that drizzles

    down dim-lit streets,

as if there were

    another way

to move through

    this place where

every hallway

    runs at a slant,

every room

    angles

toward the small

    hours.

Calling us back

Every moment whispers

        A darker blue

In these hours

        Of endless gray

Each step shudders

        On the shadowed journey

Back from birth

        As if we could ever be

Cocooned in stillness

        Each thought dreamed

While wandering

        This murmuring earth

Pulses in a cloud

        Beyond knowing

Little left to do

        But ask

The frantic snow

Triptych

That falls now

Like a stuttered question

How much longer

We need hold

To the surface

Of this waking world,

And what then

But abandon ourselves

To its flesh-cold fever

That we do not perish

It's not easy being swallowed
whole night after half-forgotten
night, lids swollen thick with kicked
blankets. No amount of fighting
will save me from sinking into
my own worm-dark silence.

This morning my breath vanished from
the pane as if I'd never been,
or as if maybe I lived in
several places at once and
had lost track of which hand carried
my coffee, which mouth spoke my name.

All that remains, a lone soldier
left by my son in the drained tub,
sword arm raised to ward off the
blow that will not come, as if we
could stand at the edge of water
and never drown.

Now begins the silent season

It's not so difficult to die.
A simple matter of stepping forward.

Fish play in a dark pool as I cry,
but when I weep the pool spills over.

I talk to trees when I sleep.
They know how to escape this earth.

I often wake to discover I'm someone else,
as if we could leave anything behind.

Once, I slept with a woman who was not
my wife. Now I can't find either.

I often take life too seriously and fail
to see that weeds don't have real teeth.

I hide beneath blankets on cold days,
as if then I'd have somewhere to go.

On the mornings I'm old, I forget the many
desires that still prey on a body.

And when I'm tired, I feel like an unfinished
room that couldn't hold furniture anyway.

Some days it's all I can do to say
what I mean to say,

body of bone, body that's home,
body that finally betrays.

[When the body forgets]

Who knows which hand
the darkness will eat first

How far the beetle's journey
over the kitchen table

How deep the sleep
of swallowed stones

What words will cross
this splotch of sun

into our infected sky

When the body forgets
its edges

you cannot go back.

The breaking of tongues

belongs to sharp daylight,   to an unbalanced season

where I am most alone.   As when a river

holds its breath   to keep from murmuring.

As when a tree   prays for a mouth

sewn shut with splinters   of the divine.

The breaking   of tongues   is necessary

when sleeping   in a bed   of shadows

where gardening   in the dark   of a decadent sun

can dig up   any number   of voices.

It means   that frozen ground   will not shatter,

that the spattering   rain   will not wake

long dormant words,   germinating   desires.

It can even   be   sorry   as when we give

in to desire   and squash   the beetle   on its back

legs kicking   ending   its petition   to be.

The breaking   of tongues   is nothing   more   than a prayer

that memory   be   merciful,   that   emptiness   fill

our field,   that when   we shut   our eyes   there is   no   one

waiting.   There   is   no   thought   but   breath.

Something like faith

Today
I woke
to a gesture
made
by someone
else

The more
I tried
to remember
the gesture
the further
I faded,
the way
evening
drains
the seen
from the
unseen
like steam
rising from
a weakened
field

How easy
it is
to forget
the world,
to forget
the spaces
between
things
are also
things

[All we know of stone]

How do you find yourself
deeply? How do you unravel
the distance between
when all we know of stone
is how hard it is to understand.

I have no gift for prophecy,
no plan shaped by palmistry
or the infinite possibilities
of the Tarot deck. Still,
there must be a way out
of this city of half-forgotten
doors, this holy building
of ourselves.

The next time you think
you hear an intruder
rummaging around your house
at night, feeling uncertainly
through the dark, remember
he, too, is only trying
to do his work, fumbling
about the only way
he knows how.

Here is the river here is the dream

The river is tired
of what it sees

of trees with fingers
instead of leaves

and cheap tricks that lead
to the sea's false song,

of mud and waves
that open like eyes

and rocks like mouths
that stutter their cries.

Here is the river
here is the dream

Watch me build
a tie between,

see as I scrape light
from grime, tear notes

from night scented with
rage and words that rhyme.

If you listen long
enough, you can make out

the loom of my heart
like a cough overheard

in a shuttered room.

What mud-drunk song waits

Let's start with the obvious:

no one wants to be found

when only dirt-dreaming

gravediggers are looking anyway.

It's better to leave simply

than to simply leave or stay

too long. Better to be a rat

crawling beneath ice-seamed streets,

gnawing on discarded hours

and half-forgotten songs, waiting

for the three-legged world

to shrug and turn away,

so you can scurry from your hole.

How easy it is to hide,

drunk on mud and blind,

so long as you believe

that you are not the hole.

A long way back

I want to crawl inside
This forest of dead
Lightbulbs, unravel
Into isn't, but I can't be
Sure the falling sea of
Voices won't drown me, and
I'm exhausted from all
The listening. The drone
Of the traffic. The hum
Of air conditioning.
The pinging of the pipe
In the wall to the right
Of my bed that is not
My bed is not made
For me is not the world
I believe in but a thing
I've learned to live with
Because I can't erase you.
Can't face the few derelict
Shadows edging inward.
While these brackish hands
Stir lies like swallows
Circling into no thing,
Into I won't hear them,
Into my name is not
This porous world where
The best we can do is
Sing back the fragments
We refused to touch.

Someone not

1.
As long as I am
A box of starlings
I will never speak the wind

2.
In the land of many tongues,
A mountain fog

3.
I step from my voice into
Mouth sewn shut

4.
In threads of rain
I cannot feel
The body's drip

5.
Like someone not

6.
The leaves are inside the tree,
The way swallows flit inside the dusk,

7.
Like the words inside this poem,
Loosening in the throat

8.
There is no longer an outside

9.
Only the bloom of jasmine,
The last chronicler of a night

10.
In which no stars appear.

[This winter bone-house]

You can feel the sleet
behind your left knee
as you stand in the field
before the coming storm,

but you can't slow rime's
creep over the windows
of this winter bone-house

or bleed yourself dry
before wind parches
the frozen pond of skin.

How quickly we fail to see
through the frosted pane,

how completely the cold
colonizes,

when darkness falls
one knot at a time

and even our cells
turn against us.

Here is the watery grave

Frigid, fog bound days slip
one against the other,

gray blanket of dusk choked birds,

the moon a diseased god
seeping through your life,

emigrant of a wordless history.

And time spreads like too many drawers,
and every life is a renaming.

Like the one in San Francisco,
driving well past the witching hour,

stopping beneath the fog line, the cold air
folding in on your senses,

the fog horn like a whale's cry,

the bellow bigger than the whale's heart
you dreamed of running through as a kid.

And now you try to imagine following
that horn,

arms great sea wings, slate blue legs
fusing to fins.

But your sadness pulls toward itself
like the fog,

and the world is not wide enough
to contain this circled dark.

Three January Sonnets

1.

This now is the hour of no birds,
the time of lost leaves and misplaced
brooms, the age of rocks that bloom
to cracks and cracks that widen
to tombs that swallow dogs and
little children who run away
carrying only a toothbrush
and a ratty, gray blanket.
This is the moment when even
the wind forgets the keys
and settles for back alleys
where, buried in last week's trash,
it waits for the end when no one
will ask it to blow again.

2.

And here we sit at the edge
of the bed waiting for morning
to kick in so we might begin
the day with the promised pancakes,
or whatever might wake us
from the sleep we never really
wake from anyway. And here we
stand at the kitchen sink washing
our forks and knives, wondering if
in some other life we might
know ourselves because the window's
reflection reveals nothing at all,
and instead of fall's mystery
the enduring captivity of cold.

3.

To have come this far only
to feel the sour pull of blood
and half-frozen mud that clogs
our wooded veins. To have walked
this road without tripping over
a single name worth remembering.
To find there is no bridge, no
forking path, only these days
crowded together like families
in a drunken holiday haze.
To know this is what we do
when our world is gone. We stumble
through this arthritic dance until
we no longer need to hold on.

II

[Why not this other dream]

Why not this other dream that limps along behind like a crippled dog? Like a man who betrays another's love? Now I don't know where I'm going. Sometimes I'm following the dog, its crooked tail wagging before me. Other times the dog follows me, dragging its back leg. I'm never sure which is which. Only that we bark at passing cars and occasionally stop to pee. If I could, I would shoot it. Dump it in the ravine beside the road. It would be so easy, the way it nuzzles its head beneath my hand, presses its nose to my crotch. One bullet and no more junkyard dances until dawn. So easy, except when it lays its head between its paws as if unable to feel.

Then today is yesterday, and I am not me. The dream is not a dog or even a dream. And you, dear reader, are not reading this. Everyone knew exactly what to do next with the lonely moon.

Someone lit my memory on fire

The tail end of it. The part that stings. The moment I remember, the flames lick away at the edges until I'm lost among dusky afternoons and   My memory is a bird hidden high, singing a song no one can hear. The crackle of flames and all that. I wouldn't mind so much except

      on the far side of the door, you lie sleeping beneath a bombed out moon. Suddenly, I'm watching over yesterday. Your lips parting as you turn to face me. Beneath a tree. A tree in a garden. A garden to which you have led me. Even a glance makes me dizzy. Then the flames burn across the landscape, devouring whatever lay between us, and I'm left wondering why I'm the one holding the matches.

The bridge

I rise from my chair and walk to the kitchen for coffee. I'm hiking the trail to Machu Picchu. I go to the bathroom to shave. I'm in a Berber tent at the edge of the Sahara, sipping mint tea. Sure, it's exciting at first. But then, I need a tool from the garage or a book from the living room, and I'm off again. By the time I get home, the best I can manage is to limp across desire. Maybe hide beneath the bridge in my bedroom so I don't hear the voices calling, calling. If I stay long enough, maybe I can forget where I'm going.

[My body haunts itself]

My body haunts itself. Or rather, the memory of my body haunts me. Like a dream that fades the moment you wake, it's there. And not there. The flash of a deer leaping across the road before you hit it. The soft small rain that falls after, erasing the lightning. The mist that cloaks the cottonwoods until licked by morning's fire. This is about you, after all, isn't it? About what happened in the past? Do you still hear it falling? The rain.

[My body faded like a shadow]

My body faded like a shadow while I sat at my favorite chair eating oatmeal with honey. No sign. No warning. Just a sputtering. The same as when I squashed my voice on the hardwood floor. Yesterday, I tossed an old letter from her. Today, a memory like a half-eaten toast. Now there's nothing but an absence. My oldest daughter has taken over my favorite chair. Evenings, my son tells the air beside his bed the story of his school day, as if he hadn't noticed I was gone. My wife knows better. "It's just like you to find a way to get out of the dishes," she says. She sets traps for the "ghost squatter," as she likes to call me. Puts little chocolates in them or sometimes peanut butter in the hope that I'll take the bait. She doesn't yet know, for those inhabited by loss, nothing fills you up.

[Hollowness seeps in when I wake]

Hollowness seeps in when I wake. I throw back the covers and grab the bedside table to keep from floating away. Something about density I've never understood. It helps to put on a heavy sweater, corduroys and thick-soled shoes. My steps are not my own and no amount of cereal seems to fill me.

The slightest wind.

The longing to comb her wet hair.

A mistake with a hammer.

Anything can lead to problems. So it's with relief that I climb into bed. Sometimes I don't even wait for night. I simply tell my wife and children that a woodpecker landed on my nose while I lunched on a park bench, pecked a hole in my head, and now I'm hollow. They seem to understand. My ten-year-old son even thinks it's cool. He asked if parts of me can break off and be eaten like those chocolate Easter bunnies.

I close my eyes and pour back in like a prayer. Dreaming, I'm as eternal as stone.

[The universe is like a corpse]

The universe is like a corpse I'm buried beneath. The more I move, the worse it gets. I try to scratch and a bloody arm covered with ruptured pustules falls across my face. So I lie here waiting. For dawn? For a rainy day? Here is my life. At least nothing can disturb me. The thought strikes that maybe the universe is going to rise from the dead any minute and bite off my nose. Its eyelids flutter. The jaw clenches behind half-torn skin.

And you, standing there with the others. You, slavering over my emaciated body. Why don't you give me your hand?

The doctor said he was fine

What it looked like we can only imagine. His body split. The edges of everything blurred. And there she is, flopping about the floor, begging him to stay, to go, as if the choice had ever been his. Like the time he was twelve and came across that robin stuck in the freshly laid tar, most of its feathers torn off before it succumbed to exhaustion. He couldn't pry it loose. It took five attempts before he managed to ride his bike over its head. Now, we watch the slick and wait like a seam sown in the darkness.

The ballet of the broken

I lost my glasses and didn't see the spider on the wall. I never saw the way it moved back and forth across the crack as if trying to sew shut this unsettled house. Never saw it stop, waiting for evening to put an end to this army of gray days. Never saw its tentative arrival at the water stain on the ceiling, how it charted its circumference like a map, looking for a way in, a safe path, the way I sit now sifting through the remains of one life or another. What is real? What has been imagined? It's like the time I could only afford tickets in the back row of the balcony. The dancers didn't look like dancers. More like spiders, spinning a dream past all revelation of the body. Which is how I feel in this chair, waiting for that crack in the wall to open, wondering what it is I see or don't see, why the obvious seems so difficult to know.

Sometimes I'm not sure what memory is worth

Lately, I've been refusing to cooperate. On those days, I even mispronounce myself. Say things like *I think I understand* or *Let's start over,* anything to avoid the absolute. It's not that I can't remember but that I remember too well. Soon we're in California, and the children are small, and the voices creep across the floor, repeating isn't everything fine, isn't it wonderful. They play so often they've become some other thing. I tell myself I recognize it. But the truth is, I don't. I'm starting to think the memory of that idea sews a skin on me each day, so if it did catch a glimpse, it wouldn't recognize me either.

I don't stay long enough in one place for it to dig the needle in or tie the knot in the thread. I've even built a trap door in my grave. You can't be too careful. Now I don't hear a thing. It's all I've ever wished for.

Peter Grandbois

To the one who no longer walks these streets

Did you know that all the nights spent with books on the orange couch or tucked tight in bed squinting by the light of the table lamp you were reading always the same story? Did you think you would lose yourself in woods spun from words until the entire world was nothing but a wintered plot in which you weren't even a minor player? Did you see how the search for the fabled spring had to end with face parched and lips pursed, unable to taste anything but your own grave breath? How could you forget to shut the windows knowing autumn arrives so quickly here? Now there's a pain in the back of your neck, a man in the back of the plane who refuses to exit, a plain of blue within the stone of your head and a knot pulled tighter than home—this night that turns inward like a flock of birds.

The veil between worlds is thin

I found a dead planet in my shoe. I felt it from the first step but hadn't wanted to stop. I took off my shoe and knocked it against a fence post. Nothing came out but a few pebbles, a quarter, and scattered memories of those I'd once loved. The sun beat down. Vultures circled above. I found a stick and tried prying the planet out, but instead jammed it in further. I peered into the shoe for a better look but was not prepared for the depth of darkness. The sun disappeared behind a cloud. A lone dog howled. I'd been walking quite a while and still had a long way to go. The sun returned, brighter than before. I put on my shoe and threw my eye to the road, knowing too well the blindness that comes before the hurt.

The alchemist is thinking of his secrets

Day after day he ponders them. What else is he going to do? If he actually spoke them, then everyone would have a philosopher's stone, an elixir of life. And he'd be out of business. We tried to get him to talk. He stares at you, and his mouth moves, but you can't hear the words. It's like they're locked inside. The sound sealed away. All that comes out is breath. People stare as they walk by. You would, too, if you saw an alchemist standing in the doorway with his funny hat, whispering to himself. We shoo them off. He is our alchemist, after all. We tried to push him through the doorway once. We thought maybe if we could get him to the other side the secrets would be released, or at the very least the alchemist would do something besides mumble, wave his arms, jump up and down, anything. The alchemist wouldn't budge.

He stands in the doorway, unable to go forward or back. No books. No transmutation equipment. It's like he's locked inside with his secrets. He's been that way for as long as we've been watching, and we've been watching for as long as we can remember, waiting for things to change.

III

Peter Grandbois

To return to things their stillness

So that we might meet at night our dead
we speak in the forgotten tongue of trees

which leads to imaginary heavens
dark as deep water or maybe a sky

without a moon where we lie in wait
inside ache dripping slow enough to hear

their silent march toward a white-throated
room filled with the rush and whir of pictures

moving like wings that imprison our eyes
with what might have been. I dare you to step

closer. You who are so valiant in your
uncertainty. It's time to face nothingness

or mercy. To listen to curses like
fire and pray the dead are dead for a reason.

Only in the dark

How is it only in the dark we hear
the language of clouds,

or in the light of day we see
the drowned moon,

as if we were immune
to that which lives inside us,

as if it couldn't one day tear
a hole in the fog–

a great blue heron rising
from the far shore of a lake,

that veil of otherness
that shapes the mistakes

we thought we'd left behind.
A part of us still moves

beneath a pale sky, through
woods where it won't stop

raining, a ghost deer running
the border between living and

every time we say goodbye.

This mad dance

How did we run naked
Through a sprinkler
Those summers long ago,
The flesh of childhood
Steeped in sun,
Knowing the shock of cold,
The mad dance after
To shed our bodies
Of the numbing rain
And how did we emerge
From the slow time
Of snow days,
Huddled within backyard
Cocoons of ice,
Only to walk to school
Like a fool going
To his own hanging.
How did we know
It wouldn't last?
The classroom's unjust regime.
The water's wintry gleam.

Sometimes I want to ask

How to believe in the simplicity of snow

When daily we stumble into rainless dusk,

The ground beneath us leathery and cracked.

It was easy then. Put on a coat

Boots, mittens, a hat and scarf, but events

Grow small. Did I say it snowed? And how we dreamed

Of walking so far into the frozen world

We'd lick icicles instead of words?

Did I say, too, how we didn't need a shovel,

Or naked desire? Only gloved hands

Piling snow higher and higher until

We couldn't feel our fingers, until

We had to dig a spy hole to discover

Our friends had already gone home.

A prayer to fall like dust in search of a home

Give the emptiness your hand.
The spider's shadow will not bite.

Listen each day for the crow to call
you closer to your winged self.

Scythe through evening's lush light
with blades of coppered grass.

Sip the dew soaked air from your cupped
hands until you remember–

it's better to distance yourself
from the world, better to settle

like song unwilling in the night,
better to cross a sea of absence,

as if you could not carry
a large boat, as if you could not

find yourself in the moon
of another, as if you could not

recall the path back to that dark sky
where your crescent voice rises within.

The way we push through light

Trees frighten me a little,

        the way they

hold snow as if

        everything happens

for the first time,

        as if they understand

how our obsessions

        seep inside until

we freeze.

        Their swagger scares me, too,

the way they ignore

        the icicle's drip,

the growing hole

        that will harden

into a pine-

        crusted mirror,

like the one in this

boundless room where

years fall like doors.

There's nothing exquisite

about the way

we push through light,

or turn from cold so sure

of itself we hear

whispering inside.

We scrabble like mice

between white sun

and white earth,

taking refuge beneath

untethered trees.

Tell me,

what I can do

to convince you

this is about snow

and how nothing is fatal

except the wind.

The color of hands

The thing about trees is
they learned long ago
how little we want to know
of leaves hidden within.

We keep the room locked tight,
so no one can ever guess
what's in the box, whether
the cat is alive or dead.

The way a dog barking
at the woods will never
reveal why, or the way
an underground river
denies the color of its hands.

The morning sun burns
through the fog, a black bird flies,
waking us with its call.
It's a good thing we can't hide
our breath from the cold.

Peter Grandbois

What the night has to say

The trees promise
to remember us
when we end

The water that is forever
darkening vows to carry
us in its hands

The earth's long arms
swear to sing their lullaby
with two voices

So little the stone
that swallows our sadness
as if it knew the private language
of pain

So great the stars
that are never here
long enough
for counting

Listen to the night
as it flies from morning
on the backs of birds

The way sky moves

Birds speak a different tongue
forged from dissolving moons,
a language that has no words
for hard love or leaf-darkened grief.

We try to translate the clouds,
to explain the rain. We curve
and dip, as if we, too, could flock,
but all we do is scratch the sky.

What we want is not what we
wanted. What we think is not
what we feel. We come here to be
opened, to taste the watery night

but find instead unutterable
words that fall like stars, that peel
away like shadows, like flowers
on uncontested wind, and bodies

that exist on the other side
of longing, where we imagine love's
brief spell lays claim to every joy,
as if bodies like birds had always

intended to slip into sky, as if
each evening we could bleed our thoughts
of the day's sins and each morning
empty ourselves of the dreams within.

Waiting for revelation

I want snow to fill my mouth in a shattering of silver, but spring
climbs up my throat with each breath

and rain shakes its back against the eternal hum until I can no longer
forget, until I stare

at the dirt-stained sludge clinging to the roadside the next morning
and remember the earth

is full of hatchings and secrets, of voices never caught in words.
I wish I could trust in rain,

trust that when night comes the soft and distant music will lead me
home. But memory stirs like crows

gathering at the river, and I'm lying in the open arms of mud.

Say it is the world

melting at the edges, or the murmuring
of trees beneath a parasitic sun.

Say it is the stagnant skin of days,
or night erasing the memory of itself,

the way our children's voices fade
once they've left home.

If we knew as much as a plastic bag
blowing down the street,

or a pie tin tied to a garden stake
to frighten the crows,

there'd be no need to close our ears
to the sound of an alternative sky

or ask why the rain must fall
with or without a storm.

Rain

I dreamt I was trapped inside a poem,
the way rain hammers against a voice.
The poem knew more than I could say.
On a field of stars not every word exists.

The way rain hammers against a voice,
we cannot translate the cold.
On a field of stars not every word exists
unhinged as we are by darkness.

We cannot translate the cold,
knowing silence is a crippled wind.
Unhinged as we are by darkness,
with tongues like little doors.

Knowing silence is a crippled wind,
we hide from what has shattered.
With tongues like little doors,
we play to keep from breaking.

We hide from what has shattered
each drop of rain a note
we play to keep from breaking.
Outside, we circle the field within.

Each drop of rain a note
we hammer into flesh.
Outside, we circle the field within.
I dreamt I was trapped inside a poem.

[How am I only]

How am I only myself when disguised,
and the sun hard against my transparent
body, and the far shore of the river.

How am I only sorry when silent,
and dusk buries itself in smoke soaked breath,
and the ghosts of letters I will not read.

How am I only hungry when falling,
and the madness of night dispelled by the
harvest moon charts the path to forgetting.

How am I only aching when inside
this useless dream, and memory thinning
to a wind that refuses to arrive.

And this slow sleep tempered by the gray dawn.
And this stillness that flies from what we love.
And this black blood that never mattered anyway.

Every thing moves toward the voiceless
boundary where we forget it is not
inside our luminous selves that we live.

So close to steam over a river

Days grow larger than trees
as you wait to decide

which window you'll fly through,
a crow across a slate sky,

until you're nothing more
than a charcoal scratch.

It is easier to love fragments
than a whole,

easier to hide parts in pockets
filled with crumpled bills

the way winter wears the fog
like a coat–

we don't even possess ourselves.

Close your eyes until
the soul is but a length of god.

What pulls toward clearing

October fog hushes the horizon
but not the ghosts needing to be held,

and the name we give to longing refers
to the many ways we can become lost,

as when the fawn follows its mother through
the sleeting storm, as when the father leaves

his daughter in the hospital waiting
room as she pleads for him to stay, as when

you tell me goodbye and I can only
shake my head no because everything

unfastens and it's all we can do to hang
on to winter leaf days. You said that no one

remembers in the end but the truth is
that there is no end to remembering

and that everything moves us a little
closer to the edge of a closed off field

where if we could retool our eyes to listen
to this human sound we might understand

that emptiness is another way to hold
both worlds, to gather what little we can.

Light water beneath the dark

On the days when I live as someone else–

a god I do not know, or a one-eyed

merchant dropping coins from citrine fingers–

I fail to feel the light beneath this buried

city or the roots from its broken weather.

I shake and shift in gestures performed by another

to rid myself of ghosts from former lives

before they carry me to some other country

where you and I read the pages of the same book.

The same life. This life.

Sometimes, if I listen, I can hear it.

The water

[Maybe only without]

I wake and
reconcile
this nothing,
as if by
shutting my
eyes, letting
my ghost hand
lead the
interrogation
I might find
the way.

How to un-wing
myself and drift
toward soundless
sea? How to fall
inside an empty
glass?

I'm done with
the porous voice
in my head.

I want to wander
the word-wood
between here
and here.

Maybe only without
a moon can we
find the unseen
shore we thought
we knew.

Sleep

The wind waiting

        outside

for an opening,

        a chance to wipe away

the anger

        storming throats

within.

        The vatic scent

of pine

        dropping down

over corpses

        of bees littering

the ground

        as if to measure

the bodies

        for the suit

they'll need

Triptych

to rise again.

The straight light

of sun bent

by the earth

until days shrink
to the leaves'

dark music.

Sleep spiraling

into flesh,

like every

thing

unseen,

teaching us

how to grow

new.

The sacrifice of things hurts at first

My steps depart from me
down avenues of banished
dead. I call out to them,

ask what world do you
think this is. Their eyes
open and close like breath

so often forgotten.

My story falls deeper
than trees, as I sit
at the edge of this loud

world waiting for the careful
unraveling of fingers,
how the end so often

resembles the beginning.

Here is where it ends

On the other side of voice.

Where the fabric of our journeys
breaks into bees.

Where the long river
of eyes.

Where we step from this dreamed
attic into woods
thin as unborn children,
wind cruel
as a cough.

We think we're going farther
than we're going

not knowing

we are the abyss
we cannot cross.\\

IN TIME

James McCorkle

The earth, now that I am about to leave it, seems so close at last. I wake, and there, so enormous in their proximity to my eyeball that I might be staring through tree trunks into an unknown forest, are the roots of grass, and between the roots, holding them together, feeding them, the myriad round grains of the earth, so minute, so visible, that I suddenly grasp the process by which their energy streams up through the golden stems. . . . I shall settle deep into the earth, deeper than I do in sleep, and will not be lost. We are continuous with earth in all the particles of our physical being, as in our breathing we are continuous with sky. Between our bodies and the world there is unity and commerce.

—David Malouf, from *An Imaginary Life*

James McCorkle

The Visible World

Here, already memory: what a word would have
been, or you, suddenly here, too—

in flight to here, but not arrived, yet
a green premonition
or, again to start: a joy to see

a familiar, a figure before flowers, gold-green
feathers, ruby throat, first I've seen here—

small joy, like a memory arcing into sight
then back into the heights of long-needle

pines, the shrill of cicadas tighten
the air, royal Poinciana flare

here in August, a wash of red. Opulent
vessels, carriers of souls, heading across the gulf—

we move in this world with longing.

——————————————

The secret to the world lies at the borders

finger laid
across your lips, pressed to where the heart lies

In the valley of forgetfulness
the secret to
the world is one among many

Seasons drift with the last
milkweed whippets
a monarch steadied on

Triptych

a span of goldenrod
knowing there are more

than two worlds in this one
field crossed by so many

The secret to the world is woven in air

a lattice of light

you walk from here
a refugee

In the secret to this world
the last ones
watch your way there

———————————————

Time measures distance, season to season's
migrations across the warmth
of the earth's body, scents rise from each meadow
along the arc bent north and south—

green diffracted to ruby, with each swerve

chuparrosa, chupamirto, chupamiel, visitaflor

cactus, myrtle, honeysuckle open to the world
colibrí carrying what has wreathed
each of us to this world, attendant to

the unaccountable, their return we would want
to say miraculous, the delicate circuits
of our bodies, of yours or theirs in the reach

of light, a flare of metabolism, aerial, heart-struck
moving in time, always into the world so fired.

James McCorkle

Drift-Lines

It is all by way of incantation
coming from a slow wave

at the back of what must likely be a form

of light, forming from blue, or
something deeper, not on the scale of visibility

what must have
a beginning, as on a snowfield nothing
has crossed
the field
all an edge of white, a shadow
crosses, and looking

up, it's a gull, a trio of them, pushed sideways
by the wind, away
from lake shore, and a further hill

a landfill, in fact, and then they disappear as
they must, the shadows
blushed into the whiteness
as thoughts that subside before
a sound, the word before

beginning, in one theory
condemnations, the history of migration from the lush
circle of trees that once

leaving
one sees only the briered thorns and twisted vines
binding sight, searing blue
above, to foreclose

unhouse, any sight
as of

drift-lines, snagging what surfaces

as of,
as of say those crossing toward Lampedusa
the sea-drift carrying them away

from sight
of land, land
-fall, of where we are, of be-
longing, each word comes as condemnation for
that loss, that unhousing
of the sky, lifting away, there is nothing
that augers hope
or that other theory, where what
comes from sound rolling, as a wave, a landfall

arrival after arrival, thinning the moment
before
the future to that opaque pane
we press our faces to, looking

for whatever might be moving toward us, as
if it were there, another word after-
wards, a light growing in
intensity, as when through a mid-winter snowfall

the sun rising across the lake, and the knowledge
of the water, the ratty grasses

gold-finches, in their winter attire
scatter out of, glad

for the sun, startled we have arrived, or
rather, come this way
after so long a quiet cold season.

May Days

The last day in May, 2007, ended with the least rain on record.

By the end of May 2007, over three thousand three hundred U.S. soldiers died in Iraq.

On the first day of May, 2010 a shopkeeper in Mosul is shot dead, part of the ongoing war violence, reported by the Iraq Body Count Project, he is one of the over one-hundred thousand documented civilian deaths in Iraq since the beginning of the 2003 invasion due to war-related violence.

May 18, 2010: one thousand U.S. soldiers have died in Afghanistan.

Sleep coils through yellowing
                    grass, walnut trees drop
their oils, soil goes
barren, the apricot tree planted last year
now wicker—
            a fourth suicide
has been reported—
                they keep them still in cages there,
across the gulf.

No accurate count of the dead
children, of the poisoning
                of wells, the infant
mortality rate that surges—the bounty of facts:

the camps, Gaza, Baghdad, Kabul are *seething*—that word is
accurate, the temperature rising
                on summer's long
approach, and the *crowding—like shooting
fish in a barrel* lieutenants say—

no one has taken yours, no one has come for you,
the lawns dry, the ground packed
         with dust, rain's vacancy.
Yours and mine have not vanished with no mercy.

———————————

Each May I rewrite this
      adding the numbers again, adding the cities

that rhyme, Peshawar
        Kandahar

hectares burning—flesh burnt off, who will look at you when you return

who will take you as a wife in five years

who will sponge your body down

———————————

Forsaken—is that a word still
to be
  used—*forsaken*,
      that moment in the valley
when the shadows grow even in the afternoon's heat
and the apprehension there is no one

left and how bread and water would be more than
splendor could offer, so what

if it could still be said, written,
that *forsaken*
     could be
       what we are.

There would be no less than that.
Finches
continue their song, thickets fill
      with what the wind
carries hand to mouth, the valleys open out.

———————————

What were you thinking, then, the grass
sere, the sky's one eye bluest in its emptiness—

the eye we pass hand to hand, that
last name ours
        sharpening its beak
to tear at us.
The Psalmist passes.

That was then. And now.

———————————

Afternoon lowers
        itself into the locust
                trees, loved ones
vanish only their bodies turn up
on the edge of highways, riverbanks, empty rooms

only their *bodies*, to say that eclipses
their wounds, what goes missing, the number
what would be sufficient now
        to say *bodies*
means *flesh*, means words made flesh

how we perish, thought
        perishes
too, with each word
and sorrow the weather of place.

Azulitos

From the window, sighting one—
thought flew out   to meet it, the desire

to see it is suddenly seeing
into blue, or seeing
blue, or from it, a scrap of sky fallen

indigo as the bunting
swung through the low branching maple, then out

across the open, an arc of blue mineralized in air, blue
this blue only for

incipient months of air-spun maple
seeds, cherry blossoms
a white-out in a sudden gust—

is it epiphany, or coincidence only, when
thought becomes
tethered, coincidence attention, still

what blue, from thought or far copse, they emerge

night migrants, without
light to diffract   into cyan, they turn

black—wintering
azulitos follow an arc

of islands north   slipping the borders

to weedy stretches of crops and woods—

arriving to this world in a moment, indigo
then gone, into
thin air, the slatted light
of goldenrod and milkweed

Measures

Overhead geese
seed
sky

so high so many

their sound falls
still
the cherry tree holds
its leaves relinquishing

no thought
of time
no measure yet

but green without the spill
of red's cadmium
spelling out

what's in the air
spinning

what is to be cut
in time

the maples' samaras

keys to that
which may
green

or the monarch's
orange and black

its range to San
Salvador's
blue peninsula
and back

(some say a soul returning)

or solitary
bee
on goldenrod

past bent pear-wood
winter will take

down
the sky then
so blue nothing will seem missing

Summer Solstice

Red-tailed hawks overhead, negotiate a thermal
that spins upward into the sky's belly:

which god's beloved were these

who asked to see too much, raiment or
ravenous for what

condemns them to flight, to new
bodies catching
light, flight unspooling always
                a meaning, sentences
pry open for what must be hidden deep inside

or moving among the greenest
greens, summer's
            face stares
out at us, in wild grasses seed-laden

and pin-wheeled fleabane
heat-ticking mole crickets and Japanese beetles
sun-drunk yellow-banded paper wasps

fire in the heat, the longest day, a young hawk
banks a slow *s*—

sound of dry foxglove and iris, milk-
weed splitting open, and the rush of lifting
           into salt-tasting heat of blue, the sky's open body—

Then, later my daughter watched
a hawk eviscerate a squirrel:

no more than six feet from them she tells me,
the whole sky empty,

bird straddling the body, pulling at sinew—
how long had it been there

after dropping out of the blue, before she
arrived, and sat to watch until backing out of the scene

not to interfere any more than she has by watching
she says—someone told me of walking in the forest

and being swept off his feet by a great horned owl
approaching too closely a nesting tree: an owl in a growth of conifers

their cones candles of seed-light, and I was between it
and what was wanted—walking alone in the woods at night, there's a path

under a line of pines that ends at a creek's ravine
where I caught sight of a long-eared owl, still

in the pine branch then disappearing into deeper woods
of maple and birch—coming in

remembrance that it appeared, cradling what I would
call and name, what it was on its way, long before and after what I saw—

———————————————

This summer began wet and cool
moving through grasses—

a spathe-headed copperhead
you picked up, neither of us knowing

even dead they still carry venom—

the world changes
as leaves shiver from green to silver

Triptych

in the wind, nothing owned—

the summer's world slow to
wrap itself in its own heat stiff grass

translates into brown-green—

listening for the hawk, pale
in the sky, spiraling higher, a snake grasping

its tail rolling in the green, a fox
rolls in the grass with the dead in its mouth.

James McCorkle

Peonies

Peonies, rain-weighted, bend
to ground—today
        a friend's child asked
who the old person was sitting there

—what can I still do, let me
enumerate the ways—
        I think of the old poets
drinking in the tea-house, late into night—tonight
the air
soft as, we could count the ways, farther into
the night, and laugh—
        the stars a burst of light—the swift
inking of a pine branch's new tip, soft
green needles

—mid-June, fireflies punctuate the nights, goldenrod
almost as tall as I am, a deer
path mazes through

in a month arrays of florets will open—days
press sooner
their heat, grass yellowing, bent with seed

news of the great fires
spreading in the mountain divides—

in two days' time, peonies drop
        their petals, strew
the path with white and pink

the last buds don't open, ant columns circle each globe
as I prune off the dead-fisted weight—

time to spare
nothing—

be certain of each cutting, each bud, between each
a calm, on and on
if we are lucky, a glimpse—someone, the old man bent over something
           as in a golden screen, seen
               in a hill-side pavilion, bristle-cone-pines
turning into a scroll, a landscape, we watch
the figure, record
spare observances: rock, gorge, pine, peony.

Cicada

Husk of a cicada on a stargazer lily's
leaf   split open   old
linen wrapper   silence wrapped around the body
before it glissandoed from itself   into the dry   afternoon

the world builds hour to hour
pitch to pitch

mourning doves nesting   in the eaves   wavering call
dry summer   thrum of cicadas

these earliest sounds I recall   and   always returning
as though through the lime tree   and pines   lifting
through a Florida August

memory works its way down to this
nothing stops its flow   until the few
things left singing   mourning dove   cicada

wet wind in the cracked-open window

keep singing after they've gone
quiet   what's seen was once seen   a thousand times

the cloud's dark bowl rises over the waters
the taste of rain before it arrives   like your lips
before you're here   before you'd ever been
the wind rummages the pines
soon   I'll be old   the taste of rain

and the doves' call—
the same pair nests here every year—
                                will not keep
me any longer than you

Triptych

your song   any longer than anything
once emptiness takes over   spreading its silk and linen

Falling Birds

after Ross Bleckner

Falling birds, falling through
their own
late bodies, through

light, to be falling

through the blue of larkspur
or paling lavender of hydrangea,

how could birds fall, fall through night
or the sheer light of day, gleaming—
is it a giving up
of the air, or muscles burnt though

to brown cordage,

as though flight depended upon
an accorded faith

that nothing would give
out, exhaust itself

and that we could, similarly

continue, into infinity what we are

———————————

In his serial paintings, Ross Bleckner's, birds
strobe white on the ribbed blue linen,

a flock of X's—torqued or

Triptych

falling stars or cartoon
kisses, smacks of white, glistenings,

a moment's gleanings, birds
twist in flight, falling between buildings, on

sheer winds tunneling between glass

or caught on the platen
an ink-jetted ghost, rush of primaries and
coverts, each a memory

flying and flown, and to lift one
is to feel someone has stolen
their weight, made

off with blood and mass and wing-bones

or to hold one
could be holding
a soul, no more or less

a tumult across the night

of migration, the movement of bodies
in the likeness of souls,

the tumult of bodies
falling across the night sky

———————————

Here in one, a hummingbird, winged sea-
horse or angel

falling, or you with wings
that are arms failing
in air

to slow the fall—here a hummingbird—here

nothing is fixed, stationary in air, or having
a vantage
point to a radius of flight, certain and then
never free—

as though to catch in motion

another form emerging
from air and fire

swift in the passage from maple to
locust,

carriers of light, each motion
memorized into synapse and enzyme
fired on a day's light
that condenses,
shortens, in summer's ebb—a hummingbird's

passage, lift against falling
where motion is
resistance, continuation's arc

across, across
grass, and gulf

————————————

Tumbling out, a memory
of flying
the room white and milky in sunlight
summer draping
the walls
cicadas tightening in the long needled pines
then ellipsis

a screening of falling, the air pulling out
feathers that drift across a blue scrim

—we can call that
sky or the clearness at morning, or
the dome of heaven—

until what falls
is a bare figure

of memory itself, the racing of blue
water, white-caps and swirls of gulls, distant ships
all approaching

as fast as a plane falls, burning, a tower of smoke
falling ground-ward, memory lasting
as long as we fall

———————————

And swarm, chaotic into one body—when a body

carries within it
what erodes capillaries and thin walls of heart
and gut

what surges through chambers

pulling down the heart's pillars, when a body
is a fragility, collecting identities
into its accumulations of tissue and sinew, and
from the heart

the lark flew, a subtle body to echo desire
of our own, as we fall the earth
rises to us,
target to arrow, the lark flew

an arc upwards as we unwind below
a scattering of trees and tiled roofs,
someone running,
a drift of smoke, everything below
unfixed, a field of places

we could fall into—

all around us song falls
bits of glacier unsealed and diminishing fallen from the cloud
the lark fell into, singing

September Notes

Cicadas unwind in the trees—
        all summer
           my daughters have collected the sloughed
skins from the cherry tree,
         split they emerged one
by one into song, tightening summer's heat day by day.

Left in a bowl on the porch steps,
          offerings to the air, the same
color as paper wasps' nests,
        they've moved on,
taken residence in the high trees,
leaves almost cadmium in the late morning sun.

In this way the world works, and beyond it,
beyond this leaving off, and wavered
transport,
     we'd like to think this, an easy passage from here
       to the there—far lake or range.

Our words drift, undulant as heat,
we hope our luck holds,
        to unwind into another day,
something better than this, though this
has been good—
     their song hovers among the trees, falling
around us all night, more and more, then not.

———————————————

The clouds are denser, droplets compacting,
        letting less and less light in, so much for the landscape
          painters with their vast golden openings.

These days allow little,
        summer is becoming lonely, a door that closed,
                a near distance, gull wheeling out and away.

And if there was, what point would there be,
        the snake pulls its last skin off before it disappears below
           ground, the deer stray closer.

In this world, we count the things
        certain—dog bark, marigold, what we said years ago,
           before this retreat and retreat

———————————————

        –thin moon,
the dun grasses heat stampeded all season,

the anniversaries we'll need to mark
from now on, a caesura widening between what once was
and the oncoming, the yet-arriving.

It's hard to know what joins
        or what is available yet
to touch, or say, some tune in or out of key,
        half-step memory,
or less, dim scent or sound, sift of ash,
the trees' swish, the moon caught there, what's
wrung from us disappears fast into hard-packed dirt.

And what's expected, to come away with something,
no raiment or array, a word before dust,
song at dusk, that we were loved,
        at least, that
melancholic settling—things on my mind,
each a shadow cutting across the lake,
there and not there,
        what we can't get past,
that same strangeness, carrying us on, too, narrowing
to a splint of light.

Hornets

1.

Stunned in the cold morning by the brush
pile, one shutters its wings
open to the early light. They are building
a nest in the eaves where the air
is still, resinous with summer's heat.
For months in ceaseless arcs from that one jutted
point of shingle and flashing
their circuit has taken them past pear
and maple trees and back
through empty quadrants above lawns.
To set off into the blazed air
was already to have returned
with what is necessary only
from the far edge of flight.

2.

Theirs is the old teaching,
certainty of destination and the exile of doubt.
Bringing back thick nectar on their wings
they carry the last of daylight
into the dark hive.
At night they strike the window screen,
the reading lamp has set them off course
and out of timing to rise
through the night's cricket-thrum
and leaf-darkness into that lit arc.
The house would be theirs if the season
did not turn, unabated they would claim
the interstices of roof and wall
and swarm the lamp until it went dark.

James McCorkle

The Saffron Gatherer

Clearing the iris bed of ragweed and strawberry runners: October
in full swing, blue crocuses flattened
by last night's rain, an arc of saffron stigmas under
petals thin
as tissue torn from the sky

or shadows of bluebirds, when what they sang
left them for the last time

nothing left to sing, sky fallen in, raw
stalks of umber and gray, seed-blown
and hollow, overhead a jet
lumbers, no place is innocent

—dig out the weeds, the thin
stem, too delicate to hold aloft

the flower's head, blue and anther-weighted
with a bee's last flight
drone, solitary

sentinel to a hive's collapse, reconnaissance
for the season's shift and drop

of light, of moving on—like everything, the garden left
untended for too long—

everything a matter of accumulation
and condensing, esters
in their long carbon chains

wrapping the scent of red, saffron, the drift of mown hay across fields,
gleaning fox sparrows.

Triptych

_____

The moon's curve rides, pitched in the evening

blue, saffron as it sinks
late (in Aleppo's foothills: evacuations)—

here crocus push tight-lipped
through clay and shale-grit, light swells through

earth, straw-stem drawn sentinels
call spring, what is dug in, corms sheathed in
brown and straggle
of roots, to set in under the cherry tree
crocus aleppicus native to the dry brushland of the Levant, white
wrapped petals
around the saffron stamen and anthers

wrapped around the desert that never ceases
screaming, the smoke from stars—

it is not possible to make the world more beautiful

in that season
when white, lavender, and saffron
wrapped

for bees, the buttery anthers
balance and tip
as the moon, saffron—
sepal to its shadowed part rides pitched

(hillsides of Aleppo bloom
once
a year, white as linen)

_____

the saffron-gatherer
reaches for the thread, red, for infusions
to wash wounds

to cure the draw of sadness the moon pulls over us
melancholy

a bath of saffron to rinse out the gouges of war

reaching for the cluster of blooms, October's light crossing over
the rocks and shadows

plucked and tied, stigmas dry
bitter and volatile

she reaches for the blooms, to spread across the bed of lovers
or weave into the sheets

stretched for love-making, the saffron-gatherer picks
at dawn, the flower

will wither by evening, when she lies down
with other women

the bitter scent of clay and saffron on their hands
still after washing

the flowers blue as the evening, pass as a flight of birds go
fast across the sea, sea sparrows

someone says, in a voice worked
down to the bone, split as dry skin, for love or war no cure.

Triptych

Fox-Sparrow

What is known, comes
abrupt, jump-cut to here, then gone—

one, banded, caught and released, was ten
how many migrations
from conifer forests south

or blown across the north Atlantic to Iceland or Greenland, scrabble
in the Orkneys, a vagrant there

fox-red bandings, with fox-gray hooding,
autumn chrysanthemums cluttered
with maple leaves

waiting for the cherry to drop its last gold leaves—

what to be attentive to
this autumn, how
to be attending
to the song, the arc before time

runs to its one last dark stop—

to pick out essential markings remembered
from the guide, is to pick out
differences, when ranges overlap

and geography is song—

Due south, through shale hills, crossing into
Susquehanna and Delaware watersheds

flare-light in the hardwoods

and tonight I read Wei Ying-wu, who wrote the jade digger
on the Lan River
sleeps in the cold thicket

conscript to dig, one from each family
to dig out the verdant
stone, moss stone, Wei watches the vanishing
river, the moon bell-struck

and the conscript's wife, miles south, he wrote in 775, weeps
in the cold hut, husband
gone for months—

in hard times, hoe the garden of stones

eat the print of a tiger in the snow

sip from the vanished river above before dawn

take from one hand and place in the other
the light of a lantern, the only gold we have on this path—

———————————————

everything travels, slippages
through shale, fissured and laced, pores of seep and

migration upwards into limestone
and aquifer, vagrant element in the rock, displaced

and shunted up, methane rings, carbon releases, condensings
of time and mass—

tanker-trucks on the gravel access roads, deep into
the hardwoods, the clear-cut for

long-hauls
to flush the toluene and radium from the wells' slick water—

Triptych

the snow starts to fall, in the high ridges
the whip-poor-wills have

left their calls in the leaf litter, and buckshot cans
surveyors' lines, posted signs shot-out

with "who the fuck cares" in dotted Morse and contrail
slash of white across the sky,

all the leavings
oracles of what came to be, passed

the one truth that continues its seep, bloodline drip, a melody
that holds a tune, one sound

the unwrapping of stars—

———————————

Wei Ying-wu whispers to me, to slip into a boat, with the early snow
and oar into the lake's long reach

chrysanthemums still bloom in the cold, come back,
show me your feelings

wine has no taste when drinking alone—

the lake a sheen of gray, early snow, geese
gray and white rise
from the waters as a single lifting
and down-pressing
of wings, like a rush of summer rain across the water

the years are migrations, each one

to the north again, the work
of creation never stops, the green half-moons scale
the bare lilac, the viburnum's green knots

on leafless branches—the fox
sparrow

lands, flying south, its song to teach to sing
no destination, only
direction, sparrow in the bare
bush, watches me, readied to fly, and gone—

a bowl of air where its song was held.

≡ ≡
≡ ≡

The Water Column

1. Snake Mackerel

From the bathyal
snake mackerel surface—

diel vertical migration
from one darkness
to another, eyes round as the moon, or rounder

    —cutlass fish feeding on clouds of luminescent squid
in turn struck
by tuna racing up
the thermocline into that sheath
of water the sun seeps through—

by then
the snake mackerel will have glided
two thousand meters down, into the cold packed water

at the very bottom of the Gulf Stream
cutting along the continental shelf down Florida's side toward Cuba

before fanning out
over the Florida Straits, and deeper, faster to the west
then up the Atlantic toward

the mare-head of Labrador—

    carrying viperfish, wolffish, hatchetfish, anglerfish
sea-spiders and basket stars in snow clouds

of detritus, as though what was found, pulled in on long-lines
meant for tuna, or pulled from pelagic
dwellers' bellies, could be only named

in our own element—
           anything else incomprehensible, rapacious
and unaccountable as one travels down the columns

tallying the nekton and flotsam, plankton, and what sinks
and doesn't, the sheen and tar, larval kills, lost generations—

along the barrier islands straw will catch what comes ashore while
those in hazmat suits scoop the tar-oil mess up
or bury it under the slender-footed coquinas and razor
clams, the grind of wave and sediment, farther out

—who knows what happens, what is there
and not—
           the day-moon half-full, begins to pull

the water out from bays into the gulf
gathering it as it swings overhead toward night-
fall, as snake-mackerel rise along shafts of warm water.

2. Oil Plumes

The perhaps is not enough

if there was wind, it would be stronger, a dispersant

it would take your face off

we are learning like an army

the skies open up

as it took your face off

egrets tissue along shore

new deployments of boom

but no respirators, they don't need them we are reassured

trees whip in the gulf wind, thin as egrets

plumes dying the downstream

reassurances stretch along the horizon, small red lights

the sky opens, it is a signal

it took your face off

dispersants spread under the tissues

egrets try to lift into the open sky its openness

3. *Pass-a-grille*

Hummingbirds return, the warm days crowding sooner
pushing blooms earlier by weeks, the anomaly
of weather, some say

thinking that's sufficient, sky cloudless, we could start to rise
without effort toward its surface
as that must be all there is

to rise to, endless in all directions, which would also
mean there is no direction
what means of navigation

past this point is there, I mean from today onwards, or
how have the tanagers
and hummingbirds steered to here

as we would want to believe it more than the draw
of nectar or magnetic bands
the slight tilt of sun to the horizon day

by day, what they hold to and amend
to reach here, where I have not
yet set out the feeders, planted the salvia

or fox-glove, the garden running downhill, still in weeds
grass-seed whips, calling back
sea-oats along Pass-a-grille—"half-way between Louisiana

and Cuba," you tell me, "griller's pass," sea-grape
and button-wood, egret-white
sand and angel-wings

all coming back, the summer silt-smell of mangroves at noon
when the day rests taut as
monofilament line pulled to

breaking, the day's hook-set in the gill plate
of a tarpon's roll and dive
the water breaks stillness then heals over, coming back

everything is the source, rising in the water
column, rising only to rise
into relation to others

drifting, medusas and groupers, blue-fin and white-tips

clouds of sperm
and egg

spawning of corals and sponges along the drift-lines
of currents and thermal
planes—one

element is another, here a red-shouldered hawk rides out
over the lake, here, then back across, one long loop
riding a thermal

higher, as I watched eagles there riding out of sight out
over the bay toward the gulf's
barrier islands—
for us, without a name what would
it be, and if nameless how would we know it to be
lost, or never brought to light—

that sad metaphor, solace if you like, or sun—
tethers
seem slipped, the unraveling knot

of name and place, thing and sound
undone, on-going—
numerous, the world a form of generosity.

Fire Regime

Recurrence, lightning strike
struck
for renewal, crack

the seed, clear the brush, for release and
continuity, before the roads
climbed into the hills

chaparral   fynbos

or across palmetto scrub,

cycles break—if there are still
cycles, if this is the way to think

about how things once worked
if they did ever
in those terms where work
is a bond
in language
accruing its own legacy, method shaping

the landscape, roads isobars
up the hillsides

————————————

and trapped in the convergence of advancing
flames
deer bear centipedes orb-spinners mice

we are like that now

keep to the walls, out of the line
of notice, sight, registration

alarms

the fire pushes us, each in our own direction, which is
the same controls, instruments
the path of flames widens

trees candle-topping

consuming urgency to continue

every season more widespread
"this is the worst" said every year

now seasons equal entire years, no
punctuating rain, heavy fog pushed in
from the coast, from frontal boundaries dropping from the north

someone told me of seeing an owl
flying from an engulfed
woods, flying and burning

reminding me of B-52s spiraling smoke
engorged over the north's rice fields cratered and smoking

---

or when she drove out of the burning tar sands
from Fort McMurray
the headlights melted from the heat

mandatory evacuations, as each season crests

in West Roxbury, twenty-three have thrown themselves
in an excavated trench for a pipeline
COR-TEN steel plates cover
sections where workers calibrate depth and passage

anticipatory mass graves was the description

where heat waves crest over and over, the land a mirage

and language becomes more exact
in its forecast
of sea level rise, fires moving through the forests, tundra burning

could burn for decades
spreading underground an intrusion

a spectra of conditions eroding
calibrations revised

she drove so quickly, at any moment she could have
burst into flame

––––––––––––––––––––

After the warnings, each a measure for the next
an emergency of slowness

is this any worse than before

I am haunted by the thought

Who counts as human? Whose lives count as lives?

As language evacuates
its own territories
who is swept along

in the rescue, in the naming
in the columns for those saved, those lost, sold or free

––––––––––––––––––––

Summer night, lawn brittle from lack of rain
codes in luciferase
diminishing
who will find each other

as you and I did, once, before we thought we needed
or before the words for this
were needed

the collusion of bodies in space, each leaning into
another

and another, the heavy pods of milkweed
the lift of goldenrod and coral
mallows

more difficult than before, disturbances
coming sooner, and leaving so little

a slippage over stones and fallen trees

all this to attend to now, a finitude, time
runs out. Something else starts.

Anthracite

Cold drives mice in.

In this world, necessity means stooping low in the seam.

No one will care, the darkness is so full
the air will kill you.

The viburnum leaves turn blood-red as mice find
their way in, the streams of frost
bite the grass along their edges.

The world's lung fills with particulates, particulars
snagging on the soft linings
tearing them

like shrapnel, a suspect
metaphor for what is like what tears
through air and flesh, to reside deep in the body.

Out of necessity

when necessity is the break in the roof

the wind fingering through walls

a stream clouded with run-off from tailings.

Necessity means dust rubbed deep into creases
of hands and faces.

———————————————————

Scrape down, or
tunnel in, grind out, all to burn

carboniferous

the laid down silt of what once lived, the black soul of
everything, of what was once

and living
and in this world no one counts the living, that I am certain of

the stars have laid down their light
into the black seams, all the pressed ash
to burn again, to burn to nothing
in the weather of fire.

And in the dark, what angels come and press against our faces
their flesh unseen
but warm, fragrant as our mothers' if we remember

or if it was, as in the dark
one is never sure, the face
so cold, wet with run-off from mitigation spray, the double shearers

tramming across the face of the longwall

half our energy there
shaved off and crushed, dragged to the light

the heavens of bees

in our dreams, our mothers bend over us, our first desires
to sing to us, to sing away
what will be.

———————————————

In the pitched dark
you want to feel yourself to be
sure you are there
not, as it seems, floating

just your thinking as I imagine this is what the afterlife
if there is one
would be, pure
thought and terror to be

in a shaft with no light, emptiness a mass
of immeasurable density

lasting forever. As might have the seams
of forests and clouds of insects
pressed to thinness, millennia of deaths in one seam, sentences

over-written until nothing that was could escape.
No fugitive

or soul, only the thin everlasting

to be burnt for a flick of light.

The teeth of the great wheels
churn through

the black, leaving behind long slots of air
hung with dust and silicosis

jackets tightening with each
inhalation. Cold seepage.

Mice in the walls.

In the afterlife. When it arrives

we will be bound together, tight as a stitch, as a seam
through the earth

bound ankle to ankle for what we have done
or failed

and our holy sadnesses thin as a seam of coal
running under

a mountain of hardwoods, whose leaves turn agate
and jasper, bloodstones, each year.

Euphrates

The date I start is no coincidence
I'm starting

Because of what is happening

I am writing it down because of being unable not to

Because the Holy Ghost speaks to the Saint

the veil torn   [September 5, 1939]

Everything takes place in a fiery penumbra, its meaning subtly withdrawn
The earth lies prey to some incomprehensible wrong

From here I can just make out the Obelisque through the colonnades
of Palais Gabriel and above

the Palais Bourbon, its needle twinned by the gilded
dome of Les Invalides.

To me, the setting represents the tragedy of a nation played out

———————————————————

Ellipsis and monument, in early spring rain
drawn faces in bus windows

whose city
whose histories

whose city's lights flood the avenues,
Constitution and Independence

anthracite dome of night
portico and pillar blanched as ribs

lawns swept of souls,
river deaf to words, the capital occupied

the fog-light of infra-red
the flare of sodium as the planet turns away from the sun

Angles cut into the night
radiant spokes

everything emanates from here
a design of matter

the stars scattered
the gods move among us

holding nightmares
waiting for us to take them

our guilt rests
a thin disc on our tongues

Nothing will save us
the gods whisper in the pines

while elsewhere planes
come into view low

and fast, concussives follow
incendiary and crushing

somewhere in villages people were eating
undressing, asleep

the air then turned to lava
the Euphrates a pink intestine, the palms

fired, burnt, the hanging gardens torn,
whose cities were these

———————————————

[the abandoned hives

no bees swarm
in the wash of sun—

what would be sufficient
is no longer possible

when, before
agate and jasper sky, world turned pearl

song washed ashore
bee-twined air, arcadia

how it began:

Gilgamesh—

I felt my soul
light as fowl rising above reeds

lion and wolf
asleep with sheep and shepherd

my face heated
flushed with anticipation

I would go to him
from Uruk shaven and bathed of the land

to my fields I would leave my soul
sparkling as mica

how it began
the heaviness of the apple and pear trees

the golden bees circling
perfect orbits

someone calling from the meadows]

The years measured by the unit of a whip
The years measured by the unit of a cage

The years measured by the area of the camps
The years measured by the area of wounds

The years measured by the weight of ball-bearing shrapnel
The years measured by the weight of tears

The years measured by corpse-fires
By the arrival of carrion-birds

The years measured by hectares of burned palms
Measured by the unit of refugee lines, the units of sorrow, of suitcases left behind

---

and Gilgamesh—

the severed head swung from a tree
midnight, stars glint as mica on the river bed

his friend asleep, breathing light
as the breeze coming through the reeds

the arc of his ax had swung
like a garland of stars to sever at the neck

the forest one, the forest itself, the evergreen maze shorn
to find at the center the gods' slave

mate of lion and wolf and eagle
bent by what he bore, asking their leave and pardon

Triptych

to no avail

_____

The earth opened, as Ovid
would tell it

as she slipped under
a burial

of her voice, into the bone-chambers underground
and from the wound, the cleft

a swarm of bees
from the cleft in the earth, a swarm as dense

as a dream, as honey
as life

_____

This was a dream, I was holding them in my hands
the golden ones, the bees still pollen-dusted

from abandoned hives, this was when the gates opened
to fire, the angels stood

as in a dream, the beginning of time
the moment we wake knowing it had begun.

This was a dream, fish heaving their gills, in
the thin burning element: I am holding them in my hands

there had been a sandstorm, this was my desert, the conditions
that we live under, we stayed up late, we could not help

but watch as it began, as it was said to have, as it was planned
the words had been taken in our sleep, sleep had been

taken: the fish were swimming in the sand
how little time there was left, the air all but fire now:

if you picture only that which you loved
could you still continue?

Method isn't communicated in writing :: Writing shows you the road taken

Other roads are still possible :: The present time might not be conducive to new truths

What would have been here before? The skin before the wound
the day before, lapis that continued into the west without end

the heart unopened, the belief in the seamlessness of life
and that movement was known and to some end

productive, a gift, a hand, would not turn against itself, we thought
what would creation be if creation is the breaking of forms

the capacity of states in their destructiveness
the heaping of books into pyres in the tubercular cities

crows rise over the treetops at nightfall
At the summit of knowledge, knowledge stops. A bomber climbs to altitude.

To block reason is to abet violence.
To begin violence is to begin time, to begin time is violence's beginning.

The dreams I anticipate terrify me :: I recall dreams I had—ruins turning to dust

[that was my dream]

[that was my dream
placed

in a chamber   (the dead are buried in their stone/chambers seated upright/rigid)
seated for all time   (what is needed/is arranged around them/They are on their own)]

[dust]

(my terror the unraveling of history
into amnesia, the severed thread

tendons, chords, muscle, you
are running ahead

to shelter
to light)

I write like a bird singing as dawn approaches
To write is to take one's leave, to go someplace else
The bird that sings, the human being who writes—are delivered

_____

moving through the wheat
entering the dreams

keeping records of those yet to be
slaughtered

every decade an afterlife of that,
compounded

not in half-lives but prime factors, branching
endlessly

_____

when he returned he was alone
he had not brought his companion back

from the world of the dead
his own want clawed him from within
like a fox in his belly

and when he reached his city he saw
it light and clear

from within its walls the sound of joy
the tops of palms green and laden with fruit

and he turned away

all that lay behind him passed from view
but for a moment

then stood still in shadows held for years

---

and in the song
cycling through the afternoon

each bird song a prayer rising
too, carried away, away

the green streak of spring
coming, we long for it

we do, we do, the bird sings
from a juniper then to maple

through the brown tangle
to the apricot waiting to bloom

on and on, profane, certain,
lyric and necessary

the afternoon echoes
high clouds

the blue spilling, lapis
lazuli, lazuli, a song

stilled on the panel, the afternoon
astonishing, still

—2006-2007

Triptych

‗‗‗‗‗‗‗‗‗‗‗‗‗‗‗‗‗‗‗‗‗‗‗‗‗‗‗‗‗‗
‗‗‗‗‗‗‗‗‗‗‗‗‗‗‗‗‗‗‗‗‗‗‗‗‗‗‗‗

Dog-Fox

In the bitter afternoon   three crows hunt
the snow-packed road   where a fox passed earlier.

From where I watched   I could not see what they found
where no one had traveled   except wind
driving snow and solitary   fox from woods
trees in black lacquer   of ice-melt and re-freeze.

Wrapped in its hunger   the fox moves past the line
of dark pines   certain of direction
the woods around him   fold their wind-guttered   messages into the air.

The snow's frail crust collapses with   the fox's headway
from barren farms   up the ravine.

An innuendo   slipping through
red-cane thickets   escaping notice   a shadow across a yard.

The fox keeps moving   knowing no mercy in the air
or its lack   gray shadow, burr-tangled
in these depleted months   meadows and yards
ponded into ice   gold leaves   blackened, in suspension—

then the dog-fox disappears   running on blind faith at the town's straight edge.

On Recollection

Breaking that day apart
like a comb of honey
            pulled from a tree at mid-winter
the tree fallen
        split trunk

wood yellow and soft—
finding what is inside
is not to be expended.

Or above, from a maple's far branch
a hornet's nest hung
            and swayed through the last
snow storm, an empty beacon,

that if we pulled it down
we could shake the dead flyers from it

like bits of gravel on the snow.
It is over soon, always that pressure

inside, that knowing which must be itself
the onset of decay,
            the mouth's thrush, the knee
cracks on the stairs,

each season offering a transfusion of light for the next,
and at night, we count
who is left that we know, the list thinning.
That lost past.

In the morning, some bird nags
on a tree—a night's waste, a night's waste.

James McCorkle

February Journal

This morning, three gray clouds, lighter against the snow wash across
the lake, rolled on, sampling the color or spread, the lake a hue deeper than cerulean

glimpsed between low buildings, that passage to here, that unwinding of some
red thread, harped muscle or chanced bones—the weather punishes us

for our thoughts, slanting in the late afternoon sun, an afterthought, or
afterlife, radiant on the snow

we would think it a beach and ourselves
stepping from the rushes, there Nausicaa or Calypso, heaps of white shells

wave-piled at their feet, but no god to turn us back to what we were, glistening
like the patterned olives we'd pick from the gulf—

no god for us, or if there was, only this
trace, *I didn't find them anymore, those lips, those eyes, that pale face*

all lost so quickly—the gods' lament (or ours),
but that would have been in 1903, overheard by a poet in Alexandria, looking

across the belly of the Mediterranean, when nothing would console, and ourselves
in another century, the oncoming of snow, the air silvering into ribbons

that end in nothing but brief radiance, the light that falls beginning in morning,
through the day, the chance it would be endless, the end invisible in its radiance.

Owling

The dark forms ‖ deer, eight step out from the evergreens

All these years, the unknowing continues ‖ a shadow [that is] myself

Anything begun provides its ending ‖ its ending necessitated beginning

The future held hostage ‖ deer in the shadow of the yews

A short-tailed shrew burrows through the snow ‖ before the shovel

Vineyard trellises bracket hillsides ‖ snow grays the air ‖ lake in distance

What color [is] grief ‖ winter wheat's gold bent in snow

Irruption of snowy owls ‖ a dip in the jet-stream ‖ lip of Arctic

Lake in distance [is] a trace of the lake ‖ walking its shore in another time

The soul, mine, yours, we've lost those ‖ the small birds left to winter

The practice of writing wanes ‖ I've left the garden in weeds ‖ deer mat the slope's ragweed

Hollows the cold flows over the animal heat of deer ‖ trails into the brush

[Is] an impossibility as it blows its trace ‖ over the turned stones

Hillside's trellises of vines dormant in ‖ the cold

Screech-owl's monotonic trill ‖ bark-gray, bark-sienna, feathering-bark

The world [is] here ‖ sounds glide over snow searching out movement below

Who is in residence here ‖ meaning you have entrusted yourself to my care this once

What would this line be without the words ‖ sound [is] emanation

Ragweed skelter out of snow ‖ chickadees bend the stiff-grasses gleaning

Deer crowd lilacs ‖ *here* designates belonging ‖ to mill, black pool, ice refrozen

Light crowds the bare tops of trees ‖ two white lines on the far-shore, hill-top, shore-line

Lake ‖ at night congregated geese call ‖ clatter of a flock lifting into the night ‖ unseen knowing

Sounding air ‖ wing to wing ‖ phrase from phrase ‖ migratory sounds

Saw-whets skirt out of evergreens ‖ *too-too-too* ‖ winter vocalization, shortening *tu-tu-tu*

Facial discs catch the sound ‖ mouse tunneling toward grasses

Secreted ‖ knot of dried snow-drops, in that

Snow locked crystals ‖ emptiness held by spun ice ‖ air falling

Carried over ‖ sparrows into the thickets ‖ open to the tangle of cross-hatchings

I've followed a line into thickets, deer-line, fox-line, hare-line ‖ who slips through, snow-bound

To the north, Ontario, ice tongues and ice-drifts ‖ push up heat against the belly of Arctic massed air

Every part of me belongs to the earth ‖ no part contraband, begin there

Basalt the common dark / in all the Earth ‖ underneath it all, the commons

Once, all there ‖ writing toward notice ‖ the there, *what was sensed*

Across afternoon's snow melt tracery of mouse-tunneling ‖ agate incursions, across smoky quartz

Walking across it, ice, the weedy ground caught ‖ all the continuity, the carrying on

Quartz and slate, horn corals, ice ‖ nothing silent, if silent, the sound we hear

Here, wing and talon ‖ vole-fit, spit mouse, squirrel femur ‖ castings

Snow squall lake snow ‖ weather-casted ‖ scattering of sparrows, chickadees, fast in their sudden

Thule

so far
there
we thought you

would never return
would the ice
sing there

past boreal
after the setting off
the long arc

of the pelagic
calling
and calling back

would ice sheet
seas
and sea tracks

mute in
north barrows
the light

of what is
out of reach but
arrives or may

in some vessel
make a long arc
coming from

the rushes

James McCorkle

rivers further silent
than their silver

scaled
windings
unknotted at the end

and then you were
not there
but far as something else

would be coming from there
willed, or willing
back

calling
though who would be listening
to it cross slate

sea and boreal
fir
coming as

a ship in wrack
ice sheathed a votive
vessel carrying

no light
its souls up-flown
the gulls white and gray

Barn Fire

Square on the horizon, the road pulls toward it,
the only certainty, hills and trees, bare

for winter, fields snow-lined, the center
all color slips into, an ark we swim to,

the local, the one word you said moments ago,
the beeches shimmered their copper-russet leaves,

the gray boards wind-carved like river slate—
it is the same story—

barn, ark, tree—you were walking toward it
the snow lit though no moon rose,

the barn darker than the sky, the trees
kept count of your each step.

———————

Wind moves through rearranging emptiness.

Stalls vacant, the loft swept.

Your breath hangs, clouded isinglass, no light

but what comes through the swung door and loosened planks.

The barn is squared on the hill, inside rough timber gives

only dimensions of the space inside, the barn's frame, no more,

the composition, what we are inside of, its limits, hold

the cessation of movement, the end of labor, the parceling

of land already freighted with division.

When the sun rose the animals were led out

to pasture or till, then slaughter, always their end:

this is the story of rescue, you said, the ark caught in a sea

tide running with serpents, herons and egrets crowding the rails,

pelicans disgorging fish with heads like sheep or horses, eels

slithered the decks—inside the painting, the darkness

filling to margins, like the sea, then pigeons clap then flash

white-gray finding the rent in the roof, passage to the sky.

————————

It is one example of what seems immutable,
but turning from it, it becomes imprecise,

having neither inside nor outside, but all surface
except for the distance we put between us,

and it, floating, a sheen of colors sinking into
each other, a field surfacing through other fields,

the darkest one, a fox runs across, a shadow
of quickness startling killdeer.

Leaving the field, a door ajar,
a mat of color all things vanish into, saturant,

and if we dipped our hands into it, they would come back
stained, knowing only one word, farewell, and turn from us

as if we were a version that could not be reconciled.
The color lets no light out. What we have is sheer presence

or the always mortal prospect of going, shape changing,
matter folding into a choir of colors, waiting for one

to draw a line out, here a tree, here a flash of fox.
Something begun again, for the moment, an example.

———————

The barn is an epitaph to the landscape,
clear-cut then abandoned
to cycles of fallow and harvest,
manure's steam rising

on ice crusts to seep
into limestone and creek-bed,

raise the beam, shod the horse
fence the fields, hedgerows

torn out for full yield
acre by acre, black-tipped

drifts, soil blown like loosestrife,
wind runneling fields

and barn-sides, writing its
runes on the wide planks

of native hardwood not found
here anymore, but after such a span

it is gray and brittle as driftwood,
quick to fire, fast to burn

like a lightning strike
in a dry field summer has bored into deepest.

James McCorkle

———————

All pitched high—
barn fire, animal salver,

first thought throw open
the doors, then

cut loose from stalls
cow   horse   pig

eyes strained for the clear
night past the roar

of grain's ignition
the door to the cold

blackness that is not
aftermath or ruins

but a cool pond
stars floated in.

And what did they see
when wreathed in fire

I ran toward them
the last one out

then rolled through the snow
while fire reached

into my lungs
burning out breath—

who was last to leave the ark,
the wife, the son, the shepherd

the same who built
the ark, the first fire

afterwards, cutting down the lamb—
last out, I heard

the animals running
into the pitching night.

James McCorkle

Source Code

Watching a hawk harried from
pine to pine,
          alighting once on a walnut's March
whip, before driven off
in the hurrying rage of crows—

hawk thwarted, centrifuge-riven into the
air's keyhole, and
watching, if the eye could calculate
its lateness, the survey

of crows, who later, folded, or fisted, on treetops along
the shore settle before the Dog Star
is out, the sky soaked in its own making,

the retreating snow, sooted
and pocked, the winter's
ruins, all a preparation for
some deliverance, an arrival,
                    decimals turning
to reach a rounded whole,

a matter of energy and matter, caliginous
wrapping around star fields,

slowing the distending, balanced against the falling
back, until, acceleration slows

but never ends. The expression compressed
to its one equation,
          the ruing of winter in the wings
of crows, the swept ground

that bare ceiling for each body's fall.

Updraft

Small deaths surround us—the dog
        lifts her snout in the wind
and rises on hind legs to
read the air, uphill, some updraft from ravine

as the trees grow violent in red and gold, sun prisms them

in day's raw intelligence, wind striping
maples, black walnuts bare as thought—
                downhill, a hare
crushed, night-kill the dog caught
scent of, as sure as the crow carrying off
the wreath of snake, cloak of vole,

and dog-fox on the ridge after the housing tract ends
parrying its kill

all logic conspires to this end
to tear at gut and balls, relinquish what tenderness
there is to the world for later

my daughter, still small, will bury her dead

as she has been learning all her life, the only religion
we'll know, its breath

on our shoulders, such a burden

light as a cat laid on the surgery's bench, breath gone
neck limp, and later the sky turns salmon and gray
as though to have nothing to do with us

but leave us on this path, this arrangement of zeroes
and ones, one or the other
allows no heresy.

James McCorkle

Fusillade

Late April snow took out
the lilac, flattened peonies
                    in the winter battered beds—

collapsing seasons, pruning lilac, green, laden
with blossoms

that later open massed in a vase, buds salvaged
from branches, opening their
casket of scents—

the old rot at the trunk's center russet
as mouth and tongue—
                              wind
could have taken the lilac down, or
blossoms' weight and foliage

noose-roped with summer's rain

could twist branch from
trunk or trunk from bore-root—

unwieldy, giving everything

in their fragrances, heart-
leaved leaf a sparrow shifts to, from bare limb
to shadow—
                    then not much, or

nothing there, the empty space where
lilac limbs were, and weave of
                              scent, the soul's weight
you said, remembering it
coming back, the soul or the body's

Triptych

parts—
          memory is periphery
the edge of things, outlines
of a laden branch, its reach, a line of geese
across the lake—
                    white underside
of throats stark against
black necks, geese
                flying in

line, necks extended
                    as to point into
time where they would
be, landing, water surging against
chest and webbing—
                    an ambit, pointing
north-south, slate-blue-to-
lilac
in the sun, slash across farm-fields, hills

to the limb's reach of memory, where
you fill it in, adding to what's been
said

already, a limb torn
blossoms cut for the table—

on the way back, a woman was cutting
blooms from a downed
red-bud tree
hauled curbside, salvaging from the storm
remnants not long
lasting, but a glimpse at what had almost been

a tree in bloom, or was
and so like, but also not

someone returning, torn, still in bloom
the shorn trunk, you tell me
you don't remember that explosive
bloom, filling the roadside, torn limbs.

May's Velocities

First mosquitoes hunger as a hummingbird, early
in its velocity passes bee-balm, globes

not yet spiked in red—
flamboyant columbine in first bloom

and mock-orange sends green racers
straight up, light as scent, the lip

of heat, tidal as summer—
against the house's fieldstone foundation

a duskywing, wings out-folded, flattened, flush
to fieldstone, I thumb the guides

and compare photos to memory, the slip
of names one world introduces another—

dreamy or Zarucco, cloudless sulfur, Horace or Juvenal—
some say this is the last we'll see

of the great migrations, arcs from Veracruz,
Esmeralda, the Isle of Pines, pilgrimages

south to north and back, migrants bringing
a song back, spun from milkweed, lantana, wild morning glory

spun from the way after long fasting, from what began
this world split from other durations to this range

and field, then flight in another duration, a single
tense I can't parse, urgent, to clasp the warm rising of day.

House Crickets

Trapped in the house, hung
to the backdoor's screen,
brown, cigar-ends, wings rolled tight
as a wrapper, but slender.
Outside, the song of others would build then drift
to a single rasp before some in neighboring trees
rise up again, as if in register with the heat,
never letting the sound burn down
to ash. How they got in, lured by moist
basins or sugar sweated from standing fruit,
through what chink, crack, or open
door, won't be known, no more than the trail
of sugar ants across the kitchen or the dry carcasses
of wasps blowing under an attic bed.

Hung on the screen, as though sifted
from their song,
nothing steals past them to signal
them to wind their one sound through the rooms,
through windows into the heat.
The relentless heat is perhaps their alarm
as summer rises like fire behind trees.
The one truth I can write
cannot be known—it remains the one word
left out, as full as the pitch of crickets
as their song curls over itself into the afternoon,
releasing its burden, which is no burden,
as the body might release the soul, if the two could be
severed, as if the body could breathe alone.

On the steps to the door lies the split skin
of a cicada's abdomen,
brown among brown heat-curled leaves and webs
spun from foundation-stone to hand-rail.

And looking closely, the crickets alighted
on the screen are themselves
hollow, perfect casts of themselves—
and what was pulled
from the body was nothing but song,
lit into the night, one
form giving into another, spreading across
the heat's expanse, the song finding
the body again,
finding joy in that one moment.

In Time

Watching, the verdant
return,
    to see, seeing, it stems
from that, occipital
lapis

lyric of rod and cone

atlas and pyramid, lobed
and flowering

I would like to think of you
arriving, in this air

out of
  seeing, then
       beside all
accounts, made
finite, and falling
     away
to you

bud-leaf and resinous
sun-gorged incipients—we could
        say all
starts as speculation
      spread to breaking

all rules, springing—
      thinking of you
in time, coming
     to light, certain

certainly, you.

James McCorkle

May Suspensions

The air carries its liquidity, gray sheen of shell
across the pines and maples
summoning
        the depleted world back,
as though to answer some question, that line
of questioning pushing against

the air, each letter straggling—
                    my daughter repeats
Bashō—morning glories
the only ones straggling to the door.

Air hung with virga,
            nothing reaches its ground,
traveling so, who reaches their home
again and again?—
                the beech's deep rouge
is shelter,
dry ground, brown and dun, these are the ends,
clutter and murmurs from above.

Kill Holes

Rabbit would be for the full moon.

Centipede for moving from one world to another.

The eagle is what comes and devours. Before you.

Lightning sweeps in the long lines of triangles.

The land slip is polished by the stone. The stone is you.

The slip is clay thin as skin. The skin gives part of itself to air.

A willow marks the stream bed. A star a dance.

To look at this invites the haunted.

The vessel has a hole so you may leave. Through it.

It is not safe to stay if there is no word for what tomorrow is.

Three varieties of tobacco.

The eagle devours.

There was once a man whose organs were spread over the ground.

A whirlwind lay next to him. His breath is there, too.

Everything is there. You are, too.

The supposition is that the vessels were intentionally broken, as a hole
in the bottom would allow the spirit to slip away

the body itself a vessel bearing sperm and seed, water
the fluids of earth, molten and toxic, mineral
and pure as quartz can be, thus

the vessel, its lines in black on matte white, trace
the flow of stars or water flows, willows unfolding,

and there is also the supposition the vessels were broken in grief
for what could hold us, any of us

in loss, nothing here, that is
seeing how fragile heart and bone are, a slip on a steep trail,
gravel sliding, as you described being pitched forward

a year or so ago, so much happens between times, when
out of touch, and now over coffee after looking

at a collection of pottery of the Mimbres, which means *willow*
in Spanish, a branch of the Mogollon peoples, themselves
named after Juan Ignacio Flores, governor of Santa Fe de Nuevo Mexico in 1712,

we know them only by what is left behind, not
how they named themselves, but what came afterwards—

you described days later the gnarling of speech, as though
a stream curled back upon itself, pooling
the sounds into a tightening silence, the heart's faltering

perhaps, the mind instructing the brain to continue
firing into the night, so then
what would be the soul, rising from one vessel or another

continuous, beyond name or place,
willow or stream-bed, coiling up, smooth as a slip

of clay, to taper into a mouth for seed, next year's
hope and harvest, and still later
showing me the apricot and apple trees, pin-oak

and raised beds for beans or tomatoes, the mid-April sun
forcing convallaria pips up, to unfurl, each drilling
a space in the air for the scent to float out

crossing the beds, the fence lines, gardens, then lift
away, as did those that coiled and fired
the vessels some say were made expressly

for the soul, to hold and release, the lines
a guide, as certain as the straight edge of the horizon.

And now—
            the cherry is in bloom,
each year I see it again, sudden cloaked-whiteness

this year
silence orbits it, no one there
the bees brushed from air,
nothing swarms—
                    stars travel
away from each other, disappearing beyond

a curve light can't bend over:

everywhere is itself, the mountain the mountain
the cherry the cherry-tree—

before there was time bees floated up
from the rain-heavy clover, cold-stunted lilacs:

then it was as it is now, except with time
loss gains, and I want to
whisper to someone, don't

tell your life, it will be stolen if you do,
then you will have nothing
                    to do but
repeat, the same track, the beat
of hooves, the god of that somewhere retreating—

the whole deep field splitting apart
granular stars pushing emptiness further apart

and
a sudden cold-spell drops
the white petals of the cherry across the sidewalk,
for a moment each a splotch of sun, unsealed

the sense it is all here, continuous

then not, not the opposite but an erosion, neurons
tapping out their signals, until one after another
misses a sequence, a beat
skipped,
a line wavers, the ghost of bees float through the cherry tree, a cloud
enveloping the tree, the mountain

the petals float up, gravity
's laws undone, the soul slips through

—the jagged hole
a vessel trepanned, the bowl broken open—nothing stays
even sweet memory, soft as a bee's abdomen, what should be
remembered is not. And that, then, gone.

Notes

"Summer Solstice": for Mary Gerhart.

"Cicada": for Ken Weisner.

"The Saffron Gatherer": the title refers to the Minoan fresco excavated on the island of Santorini.

"Fire Regime": passage cited is from Judith Butler's *Precarious Life: The Powers of Mourning and Violence*. [Verso, 2004].

"Anthracite": for Jim McKean.

"Euphrates": italicized lines in sections 1 and 7 from Georges Bataille's *Guilty* (trans. Bruce Boone [Lapis Press, 1988]) and *Visions of Excess: Selected Writings, 1927-1939* (trans. Allan Stoekl [University of Minnesota Press, 1985]) ; section 9 adopted from translations of *The Epic of Gilgamesh*. For Claudette Columbus.

"Fox-Sparrow": italicized lines adapted Red Pine's translation of Wei Ying-wu [Copper Canyon Press, 2009].

Italicized lines in "February Journal" are from C.P. Cavafy's "Days of 1903" in the *Collected Poems*, translated by Edmund Keeley and Philip Sherrard [Princeton University Press, 1975].

"In Time": for Cynthia Williams.

"Kill Holes": For Bob Grunst, after viewing the Mimbres vessels at the Weisman Art Museum, University of Minnesota. According to J. J. Brody (*Mimbres Painted Pottery*. School of American Research, 1977), pierced vessels were placed over the deceased to allow their spirits to leave through the "kill-holes."

ORPHEUS & ECHO

Robert Miltner

For Molly

Robert Miltner

Orpheus: invocation to the muses

speak to me   you gods & dogs   demi-johns & ganja sticks   reveal how alchemy charms   tongue-
tip against incisors   forming the voiced fricative then: & the narrative forwarding   incant me
to sing the crane's feather   to ink my song of loss & loss refrained   of lyrics or letters   written on
water   rune the location of a tree swallow's cavity   its captive secret an overture begun on an
island & ending under-earth   summon burrowing owls rising from ground nests at dusk in quest of
sluggard mourning doves   its call: long-short-short-short-short-short: *look   but do not   look back*

I

island

She was a girl, really, there is a double joy
of poetry and music that she came from –
I saw her glowing through her spring clothes –
and she made a place to sleep inside my ear.

> ~ Rainer Maria Rilke, "Sonnet to Orpheus II"
> Translation by Robert Bly

His praise was as if in a world of as if.

> ~ Czeslaw Milosz, *A Treatise on Poetry*

Robert Miltner

apple trees in bloom

a satyr walks as easily as a bee legging pollen   a whited path transects the horizon   tiles rouge across the farm house roofline & the stone cider mill: pippins to *pigeonnette*   russets to *cloche*   & look: an estate is a plan as strict as a scripture   there is neither inkwash design   nor rook of black ink streaming tattoo shadows   nor action painting   nor watercolor blur   nor black & white photo transcriptions of the provincial road down which that satire of a centaur   goat-legged & chrome-horsed & leather jacketed   ended idleness with a deft touch of a cutpurse   Eurydice stolen away on a Victory motorcycle   sound storm to dust cumulus   & then a silence so stark   birds dared not sing   so Orpheus was left   lost   down the fence-lined espaliered lane   of a red-roofed domain   wandering the distance   in obscure movie camera moves   as if panning the grove's rows   zooming & jump-cutting   perspectives luring Orpheus   into a known canvas   as uncertain as the roots snaking under the copse   & so up reaches Orpheus   to gapped & glinting intervals of refracting light   to boughs laden with thick-as-paint brushed blossoms   once the French doors greened open to him   arms wide & wanton & waiting   once the bridal path was embroidered anemone & narcissus   once the gravel walk was well-swept   as a good translation

Eurydice: symphony in green & gold

a vague figure: a woman   wandering solitary on a wooded pathway   entranced in her own reverie
a shimmering of delirium & daydream   lost in thought on a known route   every fancy catches
her: finches in birches   delphinium blooming at field's edge   & damselflies dancing impetuously
in sunlighted patches   dried stalks remind her of milliners' straw hats   & a street vendor's
leafgreen shawl she bought last week at a crossroad market   how she revelled   delighted in its soft
fabric warming her arms   as if paint brushed upon her body   no magician could out-marvel
look: across & over her shoulder   a pole balances   with a *japonais* paper lantern   suspended as if a
bee skep   as if a wasp's nest   as if a skein of wool   as if cocoon enwrapping the psyche of a
lost lover   she's inclined to find fancy-freed amusement   as if a crow in constant quest of luster
ideas swarming as if golden orchard bees   come dusk she will be mesmerized   rapt by
constellations of fireflies   as if stars lighted by comets or a sprite's taper   or candles set in cropped
grass illuminating her way to Orpheus   she's not content to read or play lute   she'll rove stand
& copse   catbird meadow & peregrine creeks   until sun runs   until crickets click   until a moon's
a broken clip   until clouds wisp as if a pipe's ribbon of smoke   night for her is a necklace:
a Venetian brocade   or a silk & pearl evening dress   to match her infatuation with darkened places:
grotto or closet or culvert   stone well over an aquifer or underground river   or a burrowing
owl's underground nest   Pandora places where   oracles the fortuneteller   Orpheus cannot find her

water lilies

three amused sisters   sit in lotus position in the center & bow of the small boat   into the pond I
row   lilies carpeting its surface   the girls' straw hats & bonnets with green bands   mirror
the surrounding morning blooms they've pulled from the water   filling the boat as if a gift basket
& lily pads as if wedding plates   yellow flag irises are raised   as if champagne glasses in toast
to the sisters' sumptuous lives reflected on the pond's surface   I am neither bridegroom nor gondolier
rafts man nor ferryman   merely one of strong back & sinew as if rope   with bending branch
arms & owl's neck   I propel us crab-backward   my spine my eyes   into an un-thresholded future
midway I pause the boat & we are as suspended   as are insects sealed in amber brooches
pinned to buttoned high-collared blouses   & so paused we blur: pixels & broad brush strokes &
color hues   creating depth in a moment's space   where water & land   women & flowers
intersect   the wind's eye closes into abeyance among birch branches as if chime & interlude
afternoon light fractures & glints the mirroring surface   our faces hesitate & lapse   so that
commas & caesuras hold us   as in a sepia photo: flyer & voucher & leaflet   tacked into a tableau
below the surface   then I propel us   toward distant white & dappled willows   where order
is disrupted   bright the day   warm the sun   soft the wind   slow the boat   calm the lily pond
under half-opened parasols   the three sisters   un-pin & shake out   quarrels of cave-dark hair

coincidence of distance

Eurydice in the rain: her hands held upright   her fingertips interspersed   among passing &
splashing drops   she rubs as if weaving a shawl   from glistening silken threads of falling water
she cranes her neck   & raindrops run down her face & shoulders   back & waist   legs & knees
her laughter is liquid from an excess of intimacy discovered   in an interplay   between body &
water as she feels more dryad than wood nymph   so suppose she is a wren   a cupful of feathers   or
a walnut shell-small nest knit by a hummingbird from gathered spider webs   Orpheus atop a
ledge: perching where a mountain stream spills over the stone limen to a pool below   *if gravity is
science* he thinks *then balance is an art*   he hears a pair of canyon wrens with their golden-throated
tone of rippling intertwined notes   then Orpheus turns around   & looks down   he sees a sapling-
slender woman   lithe as if a willow branch   flirty as if a damselfly   she is a rain shower slow
dancer   she is the *tsk tsk tsk* song of the silken-tailed waxwing   & she is as if a sprite playing a lyre
of white water along the xylophone spine of Orpheus: shudder & vibrato   tremor & fracture
quaver & quake   while distant Aeolus paper-combs cedar foliage & aspen branches & birch catkins

idleness & indolence [love song]

summer morning slow time   the quiet of pillowed beds under canopy & branch   languid touch &
solace   Eurydice ungarlanded reclines   an intimate & indolent oracle   between thumb &
palm she crushes thyme & marjoram   works them into my hands & fingers   so they can strum &
pick & dance & chord down the fret board   to the guitar body   where secrets sleep in abeyance
& music waits to be awakened   my hands braille in return   I am trellis & she morning's glory   we
are grafted trees of apple & pear   entwined grape vines dreaming wine   her voice is as if leaves
of aspens   as if water over creek rocks   as if wings of gliding seabirds   or Icarus flying toward a
citrus-colored sun   insects buzz as we drowse   the air seems as lush as caravans newly arriving
from Thebes or Cathay   exciting as the round & plum-soft tannins of her breasts   lush as a raspberry
finish long as her legs   or the luxurious lingering on my lips: sticky clover honey from wild bees

shore line: epistle to Eurydice

textures of letters clamoring to be poems   postcards   ransom notes   nom de plumes   or traded
stories   as if pictures cut from glossy magazines & taped to a door   each typewriter key
peppering song lyrics on a page seasoning folders   to hold a reserve of sketches & word lists   as if
ink   as if type   as if charcoal   fragments & shadows & flying fish swim past birds & walls
bend to intersect ceilings   see a sky reflected in a pond: an arrival at an ocean's liminal edge where
tides are pulled toward a crescent moon   where dark stars & black holes & quarks   are
undercurrents of an invisible universe   wave & particle expanding & colliding   whitecap & crest
& whirlpool of bed sheets   a lapidary of lovers   as a river's mouth kisses an ocean body   where
a beached starfish is want beyond bearing   where waves erase & rewrite our names on beach sands
inventing tales & myths & love songs of how I am salt sea   & you a shell held to my secret ear

portrait of Eurydice as charcoal sketch

written in runes: the wish girl charms   feathers as if a scarlet tanager or winter wren or vermillion flycatcher   drawing me into rooms and canyons inked black   where shadows slate walls & cliffs   as if tattoos written on cotton paper   & this island hummingbird asks me what kind of songbird I am: goldfinch or meadowlark   prairie warbler or orchard oriole?   imagine I say I'm a school bus of open beaks   a jazz band of bobolinks   an aviary of titanium tin whistles where world is whorl is word is letter is poem   written on an open origami palm   & skin is paper is tale is taloned dream song is a stylus sketch of deranged cages   with her hands as paper birds

coincidence of direction

give me a brass compass   a magnetized needle afloat in a bowl of seawater   or an antiquated stellar astrolabe to point me away from the direction that leads to my demise   I am a disuse of sail & paddle   a rudder redacted & ruined   leave me a raft caught in a trough   or an orphan in a kelp basket   as if turtle or waterfowl bereft of water shadow   can you hear me silver dollar sliver of an ear?   do you see me waxwing boy soon known to sunlight?   among whitecaps & cumulus clouds I am but a minor planet   a pear in an apple orchard   or a plumb bob pointing to no known plane where chance & dispatch balance   so with the oak barrel merit of wine's alacrity & excess   I recite this sober poem without guitar   as if overture is sailboat is island   let me be aperture & harbor

adrift: a draft

not a shipwreck   not a beaching   not a running aground lost & found   but a seabird siren-song
see the sailboat cast off its keel & tiller   sail & rudder   growing two oars changing into branches
that reach & grasp sand & hold the hull from bow to stern   as we turned into jettisoned yellow cargo
& bleached driftwood & maroon castaways   we knew we were water   knew signs & signifiers
knew how meaning is gleaned   from comets & stars appliquéd on black velvet   an epistemology of
light absorbed behind shut eyes   so we dreamed we ourselves were the island itself: vale & fen
hillock & stream   some round sandbox stranded in a room of white ocean   crowded among tortoise
& terrapin & spotted mapped turtles   each shell a construction of reflecting moons   waning
& malleable   adaptable & waxing   & from distant Samothrace we heard both mockingbird &
waxwing calling   so to starboard we turned   held hands   held breath   as overboard we dove

Eurydice rising

a woman I loved   among yellow pears   fell in an orchard of clapperless bells   gravity loosened the
grove   snapping stem from branch from tree to ground   & in her trembling   we tumbled free
until ground grasped us   clasped us   & broke our fall   bruising her & bruising me   each of us
but damaged fruit   perfect only for porch or church or cider press   we were seed & skin
nectar & juices   dreams at a garden's edge   where our enjoined hands released   & up we dove
through foliage   ascending staircases of trunks & branches   emerging from the lapidary of
leaves   our faces uplifted skyward   reflecting a waning morning moon   & as we bid *adieu* to the
obscure light of loss   we embraced roughing winds breaking & cresting the ripe fruit's golden
patina   as I turned to see a wren I heard   she climbed the horizon   the wax still soft on her wings

epithalamium [dream song]

the same dream visits Orpheus: alone in an autumn orchard he walks   moon-drawn through
shadowed labyrinthine rows of trees   stopping at unintended intervals by the scent of fall's
ripeness   his fingers slide the firm skins of apples: honeycrisp & ambrosia & splendor   Spartan &
Faust's winter & fallawater   beyond an espaliered fence   Eurydice sleeps on the ground
in fields lush with lavender & marjoram   tarragon & thyme   as he enters the dark-winged dream
Orpheus watches himself   slide his arm under her head   his large hands cupping her tiny fists
as if they were stolen   lemons or Clementines nymphs appropriated & absconded   he'll hold her
soft as marmalade palms   wrists thin as sticks   fingers as if candle wicks   until loss & lack
rescind   & Eurydice rises into night sky   shawled in a moon-frame ocean-white as if a wedding veil

alchemy calling

August bakes wheat fields into leavened bread   storm clouds brood the horizon   the sky seems
overrun with centaur spark & dragon smoke   urgency traipses as tinsel disaster at the intersection
of cross-purpose & crucifixion   fool's gold & iron transforming into precious metal feels medieval
in the collapsing world   where lead-cast children anticipate metallurgical rapture   as if dolls
nostalgically dressed as dead saints & rotten gods culled from catacombs   their bones hollow as if
bird's legs   through which air whistles & whispers & wonders who   at that crux where wheat
& chaff meet road   will ride dark-winged Pegasus from previous to present to what's possible?
as telephone poles topple dividing lines fail   the cellphone tower replacing them appears as an
aluminum finger   a hand-span measure of breath & motion   pointing toward gusts or ghost dancers
as a static of sparrows & grackles & jackdaws cracks silence   Orpheus listens   laughs   tunes
wound brass strings of his guitar to the Aeolian scale   his fingers run down its backbone   across
neck frets   as if drops of hot silver   as voice is song is loaf of bread scented with gold & honey

Robert Miltner

Eurydice waiting

a small woman in a long golden dress leans against the dark wall   her right hand rests against fabric
her left hides hand behind her back   while she waits she poses   as if an actress alone on stage
of an empty theater   illuminated by a lone stage light   her off-the-shoulder dress with its cleaving
chevron makes her neck seem especially elongated: blue heron   borzoi   gazelle   detached
chalice   estranged & floating   in the atmosphere of an otherworld or underworld   seen as if shadow
& shawl   she's a faceless figure foregrounded   as if a waiting paper doll   cupping hope in a
hidden fist   she leans & listens: no birds sing   she leans & wonders: is that footsteps' percussion
calling & awaiting?   a rescue song response from Orpheus?   or is it only her heartbeat's echo?

three gossips: ballads for a blue guitar

first

I heard he's impulsive   given to child-like tantrums   crazy as a grounded bird   drawn to haunted
whorls & spinning to flawed excessive fetishes   some say he's senseless as a hermit crab
unshelled   a tarantula withheld from web   as a man with a separated head   as a writer without pen

second

well   I heard he was a melancholy child   all broody & brainy & mysterious-like   & how he still
believes   in luck & miracles & aubades   they say he dreams he flies over the city as if a bird
as if an air traveler   he says he's un-homed   says to own a house is a lapse   a lack   a lessening   or
a loss   so he's given to immoderate fantasies   & left defenseless   everybody knows he's
explosive   animal-like   animal lithe   lithium to fill his private life's sink hole   he's broken   it's
said   from a baroque pursuit of bodying onward   so he feasts & writes & rants   fights &
prizes a stolen woman & lover who haunts: a loosening   a leaving   an un-leveling   an un-living

third

& I heard he's a harlequin   driving a mobile home   a bird coursing over coastal cites   dreaming
of seasonal delights of provinces   inlands & islands   lighted cities where mannequins measure
their lives   once by twice   oil lamp by black hole   dance partner by despair   nasturtium by guitar

II

studio

Yes! radiant lyre speak to me
become a voice

       ~ Sappho, *If Not, Winter: Fragments of Sappho*
               Translation by Anne Carson

Mockingbird, can't you see?
Little girl's got a hold on me
like glue
Baby, I'm howlin' for you

       ~ The Black Keys, "Howlin' for You"

studio session [sound check]

amps: a skyscraper Marshall stack   like Jimi Hendrix had at Electric Ladyland   when he recorded *And The Gods Made Love*   guitars: Lennon's Rickenbacher twelve-string   Blind Boy Fuller's National resonator dobro   & the 1960 Fender Stratocaster Duane Allman played at Mussel Shoals acoustic guitar: restored C. F. Martin dreadnought D-28   keyboard: Farfisa Compact Duo with foot pedals & Leslie amp   percussion: vintage Yamaha Digital Rhythm Drum Machine   flea market Cuban maracas   bodhrán & gypsy tambourine   roadies: the Titans   backup singers: Circe & the Sirens   Calypso & the Centaurs   Dionysus & the Three Dactyls   engineer: Zeus who demands: *has this damn album got a title yet?*   *torn apart by love*   says Orpheus & Echo says   *torn apart by love*

summer's ending [song]

an orange beach towel covers   a white bathing-suited woman   it wraps her legs   hoods her head
& allows her to stand facing the afternoon sun   yet it doesn't stop the off-shore cold winds
her sand-brown shadow   collapses beside the raised hand   shielding her eyes from the pale clear sky
other bathers gather shells   as brush strokes of cirrus clouds tier a sky   that won't warm them
on the strand   fallen cottonwood leaves   skate over undulations of dunes   as if a shifting season's
loose change   out past the ragged stands of willow   the land levels & farmers cut cornstalks
for silage   vintners gather sweet late grapes   & in orchards   last apples gathered from ground &
branch await the cider press   one morning snow arrives & dervishes & drifts   as if an ocean
of white-caps   flattening to linen & dun beaches   where a motionless flock of monochromatic
seagulls   held aloft by the brisk headwinds   flap in place: a tied string of origami marionettes

snow at Louveciennes & rain in Arles [song]

the world is an iced cake waiting to be sliced   trees blur into a tableau sky swaddling them in whitish-gray mist   a woman moves with care along the village alley   her boots slip on uneven paving bricks   yet her umbrella is as serene as a cathedral dome   she stops & looks   at boot prints making tracks in the cinder lane   she stands enchanted   by the wondrous ice contours   hanging from a stone shed's decorated eaves   snowflakes accumulate & drift as if possibilities   March snow falls heavily   sponge-bath cold as water straight from a pump   frosted are the dormers & dark the woman's hair atop her cape   she is as if a tiny doll in a large box   as if a murmur or whisper   a hush or a stillness   or a forest meadow at midnight   the woman's vague figure approaches a simple green garden gate   as old & mysterious as a wooden door   behind which lost spring ghosts & idles

Eurydice: coincidence of remembrance [dream song]

how will you remember me   my Orpheus my songbird?   as a fledgling fallen from the nest?   as branches holding you as you healed?   the garden where your face was a sundial?   as a blind sculptor who could rebuild you   by memory from clay?   as the rocks you broke yourself against?   I was your doorway & roofline & bridge   I was your sunrise horizon   remember me when blue herons fly south   when bees ready hives for the fall   remember me one winter-weary April day when the windows & the French door open again to let in arriving robins   I'll be the waxwing hovering   over golden apples in the autumn orchard   its song echoing off tree trunk & canopied branch   I'll be the lone coot call that resonates at dusk across the surface of the lake   I'll be silver minnows seen darting where the river riffles over rocks   I'll be daylight's last flaring match   & I'll be a soft day's rain   filling the birdbath or champagne flute of your astonished open mouth

Paris: ghost of a chance [unrequited love song]

Hellene: one look at you   & a thousand thoughts launch as if space shuttles   in quest of the lost object of my obsession   I am a sad linguist longing for a lapsed language   I encode desire in the words I choose *not* to describe you   in ones used overshadowing those hidden   if only I could open you envelope that you are & read your secret diary entry   me the brass key sneak   sticks & leaves & stones   with bark & twig   I work & weave songs about you   for you   to you   my odes are everywhere   indistinguishable from the tendency toward nature's cubic perfection words that hide in root & branch & trunk are resistant   they live there: I release them   set them free   do you see my poems in the bird's nest   my lines a flowering tree branch at your feet? all those hours I stepped off haiku in snow   my lonely angel shape an impressed illustration   rocks spiraling as if a snail's shell housing   my awe & my agitation   my ague & askance eyes   & couplets I conjured   carved into tree bark & floated down the creek & past your feet   bearing enchantments?   or were my failed sentries only stones & leaves & sticks?   Hellene: heroin ghost dancer   invisible layer of inked notes scribbled in the margin   how you rune & mesmerize me   so daunted & abashed   how I wish I could foray you at close quarters   you: an astounding tower   me: the pepper canister bomb coming over the top of the wall   walking my dog to avoid suspicion I pass your house nightly   TV blue windows I watch without blinking   what color your eyes?   brown as soil or sand?   blue as lake or sky?   green as if an echo of distant trees?   black as tattoos?   & what is it like to be inside your house?   to be inside you looking out?   wanting in turns me inside out   & does your husband know your heart   that robin inside the ribcage?   or does he frame you on his wall?   I imagine you more darting goldfinch than mourning dove more bags of bird seed than of breadcrumbs   more road song than going home   Hellene: incantation prayer   chant   ritual litany staving anxiety   dimming candle against the night   what's to become of us?   is the voice I hear yours cloaked in my own?   are you the *I* heard when lights flicker & what's inside spills out   as if an inverted paper bag   emptying the contents of its nothing & all in a pile   as if pollen for a bee to bumble?   as if a letter O & a zero for a broken poet to inventory loss refrained   Hellene: oracle   crow shadow   ink decanted from grape skins   rice paper yet untouched by a calligrapher's brush   facsimile & fetish   how you derange & mesmerize me with your astral body   you: a quark & a dark star   you: redoubtable & coy   me: qualm & talismanic

Cupid & Psyche [love song]

Psyche still dreams   though I've been up since the just-dawn   her body is erotic geography   a pale
land where I arrive as a phantom   a ghost   a corsair   as she reclines on the bed   as if she's
an inlet   an isthmus   a peninsula   & when she awakens she'll wonder: why do my lips hum?   &
why do my nipples rise from the areola as if hilltop temples?   quiet as if an arrow notching its
bowstring   I will steal into a brightening morning   where a risen sun lights the smirk on my face &
I will laugh   seditious & naughty child I am   for tonight I lie with Psyche   my lover &
obsession   as lusty-eyed Venus   pasted bright & aloft in her rightful elliptical place   among planetary
bodies   will jealously wax white hot   seeing Samothrace island   holding two entwined lovers

green door [tone poem]

from among flowering branches a face emerges   eyes as if apple blossoms   cheeks the blush of
cherry boughs   mouth as if a red bird's wings   dawn approaches the French doors   opened
wide as if waiting arms   & offering impressions of genteel idleness & indolent silver ease   draped
in a pink shawl   & holding a cream-white parasol   dawn lifts her dress & golden slippers to
step over the pastel threshold   as the lemon-yellow sunlight carpets the oak floor   rendering a soft
glaze on the rough wood   a porcelain vase   set on a table   embraces its sumptuous embroidery
of hollyhocks   & in the gentle breeze   the boughs of pear trees wave   as if wings balancing &
folding   while wisteria tresses trail   the red bird opens its beak   as dawn begins her green song

painting the town wine [cover song]

tell me why we fooled around   one night at Café la Petite Coquette   how our words were flirtatious
& lighthearted   as if hummingbirds   hovering near trumpet vines   in a meeting of beak &
cochlea   how dalliance drew charcoal sketches   of Sirens playing rock guitars   how seduction
enacted campy romantic overtures   so we wrote whole new alphabets   using stylus & crane
feather & grape skin   aiding & abetting   our amorous adventures   so enchanted audiences   could
strut & swagger   as if roosters & hens   how we broke the cockles of the arts   we were riling
cracking & reconfiguring   both code & codex   so we could be genuine & generous & gorgeous
as if a collaboration of cockleshells & charms   standup & shout-out   low bows & high fives
how we sassed & seized   our poetry as if some red red rose   & our prose foolish & playful coquetry

Narcissus Boulevard [selfie video with soundtrack]

see   here's the thing: I am ocean's grandson   birthed by a sea nymph   son of a river & a monger
of shellfish   tongue is the oyster in my mouth   pearls are my eyes   fluid is my movement   so
from sediment I speak   & from a diamond sparkle on the sunlit surface   I know I am Coco Chanel
& Cristóbal Balenciaga's love child   you call me a costume but I'm a moment's man   a fashion
movement   a monument to personal style   for first one on the catwalk is last one in memory   line
& circle is cheetah & leopard   leg & ankle in step with foot crossing over foot for flow   I'm
always marking where I am is where I was   is where to see my shadow   stride & turn & return
arcing toward the runway's end where I pause   pose   pivot & land   not home in Thespia
but in the thoroughfare or throughway   I'm a nonpareil   an exacto cut design   appliqued on
newspaper & glossed on covers of magazines   a scarecrow in a tuxedo   stick man with a
stickpin   draped in fabrics & leathers   strolling the sidewalk   as heads turn   knees joint   hips
hop   & long legs skip-dance   up staircase   on landing   to balcony   mezzanine   & to
atrium   & I arrive   on rooftop patio & bar   the sun my spotlight   bright bursts of noonlight   as
if camera flashes illuminating   glass block by city block   reflection mirrored on polished stone
of department stores & windows   refracting as it enters eye   forming an image of myself upon my
retina   O the wonder of such a copy of my likeness   a razzle-dazzle phantasmagoria   the
geometry   the very glory of a hundred pictures of me   simultaneous & sensual   miracle & mirage:
Aphrodite shapely & Ulysses uniformly & Achilles architecturally   like my legs I like so much:
ash & oak & poplar   & my hands as well: vines & fig tree branches   against the grimace of traffic
jam   I'm smiling at streetlights   & preserving my poise   for the politics of sidewalking &
whirling in O that red red shirt   & being seen as a human being   not some beehive drone among
the throng   me humming electrically along   as if I'm my own homo erectus cellphone tower
O I am as much a wonder   as seeing a sky filled with cloud statues   observed floating on the spring-
fed lake surface   in the downtown park & gardens   suspended within a meadow's surrounded
spring bounty   displayed on its beheld palette: jonquil & daffodil   daylily & hyacinth   narcissus
& wisteria   lilac & iris   as bright as eyes can conceive   have I become Paris   in thigh-tight
slacks & suede blazer   boot heels making the stone path sing?   O how different & divine a human
form am I   rejoiced & reflected   in both window & water   image & eye   there: it's me   see?

clatter of jackdaws: portrait of Eurydice as a sorry sight [alternate take]

sorry knocks on your closed door   she tells you about a rabbit hole of orchids & opioids she fell down one day   about the motorcycle sidecar she rode off in   sorry says *I'm no-show & heave-ho & go-go*   you're the tarot card torn in two for joy   you can't song & dance your way out of this mess sorry stays for breakfast: sourdough toast & sorrel marmalade & sorbet lattés   no sparrow no crow   only sorrow: three for a wedding & three for a charm   sorry says *I'm scarecrow & cockcrow & escrow*   you're foretold & forlorn   solo & sotted   sorehead & soothsayer   you're four for a boy   sorry forfeits forever for evermore   forks over a fiver of silver   you say sorry's a sorrow say she's your grief   your heartfelt & heartsick   your anguish & ankle bracelet   your woe whining like a blown engine   your sixth sense you can't fix   sorry says *I'm presto & whoso & shadow* sorry's the seventh secret   dressed as a deception   hidden inside an off-rhyme   she's betrayal performed without intermission   you're a sorcerer denounced in a dunce cap   a regiment of regrets an eighth of wishful angel waiting for the elevator to the afterlife   sorry says *I'm Velcro & lasso & yo-yo*   sorry has a wired sense of jest   just deadpans & puns   & self-effacing jokes based on her own nine names   but she won't kiss and dwell   she's no doorbell   no dumbbell   sorry says *I'm outgrow & nouveau & bye now*   sorry is a sonata not some shabby beggar   you'll miss those ten birds leaving the nest inside her chest   that clatter of jackdaws & ravens   each as if a cold crow to count on a bowed phone line   each a note perched on a music score   for a tone poem on sorrow

portrait of Eurydice as theater & thespian [dream song]

imploring a possibility to release me   from a probability of living inside a tin cage   I hear the clasp
release   clack of beak & wing-thrum: call it a jail break   a flawless nightjar flight   from
island to archipelago to apartment door   arriving feather-beating   & standing with knocking hand
held   as if a flash photograph of a fist   so a portal opens from threshold to theater to ticket
window to stage to green-eyed Eurydice   she's a hatched constellation   of catbirds & mockingbirds
on a liminal catwalk   over black curtains parting   heights where gravity arcs the earth   where
waxwinged Eurydice swings & gyres   on a spider web-thin wire   as the house light dims to darkness
outside I am Zeus-silent at the exit door   I am Circe-encircled by opaque night   I am as
unsuccessful as falling Icarus   I am as undone as if a broken locket   that un-holds Eurydice's picture

number ten [fantasy]

dear you: I was so removed I was a dark horse   a yet-to-be-named planet   incalculable yet not
infinite   no wonder I was ripping curtains off the windows   making repeated cell calls   oblivious
to how they were placeholders   obvious intersections of multiplicity   as if prolonged promises of
moving to other cities   where my reflection   disappears in store windows   I wondered why I
was an unknown   a riddle at the point where a millennium   turns a turnstile: exit & entry   yet you
knew   the spot to dig for bordered treasure   knew the *you are here* axis   October: a number 10
envelope arrived   addressed to me   naming me by no name   how could I tell you who I really was?
to myself I seemed the sealed book   a locked locket with a lost key   yet through the power of
magnification   I discovered theories of myself at my worst   let's suppose we awaken   on floor or
shore or futon   & you whisper this secret: *desire is memory of touch of skin*   let's suppose we enfold
neither as explication nor as exegesis   but as portals of promise   as if letters undelivered & unsigned

portrait of Echo as Camille Monet in a red cape [song]

do you see me now Claude?   I am red as if a scarlet ibis   as if a rose finch   as if the ruby throat of a hummingbird   see how I loft as if a medieval cathedral   my spire scraping a cumulus cloud sky   framing myself in these open French doors   I arch my back as if a bridge   as if a figurehead of a sailing ship   arriving in an island harbor   will you give me Claude   half the attention you give your canvas?   a woman's body   is threshold & sill   lintel & gate   an orchard dreaming fruit or flower   Camille Pissarro tells me   how my eyes remain lovely still   that he sees my old self whenever I smile   but you Claude make me feel transparent   as if glazed panes of a glass   as your gaze goes through me   from the bridge you look past the lotus lily pond's surface   seeing below only mystery & immortality   yet I stare deeper beneath swirls of goldfish   & all I can see is Ophelia

lost at sea: Hart's song

when the fall finally ended   you wanted to slow things down   so you booked a week's cruise in the Caribbean   drinking mojitos at the unchanging pace of tropical skies   salt rimming the glass was the color of beach sand   & the darkness following you groped noiselessly for your lover   too bad: he was stuck in some soggy Midwestern state   feeling sorry for himself   as tediously as the endlessly rainy days back there   so you watched the wake   the liner etched into glass-flat water with retrospection the minor key you kept slipping into   while pre-recorded reggae & calypso tunes   piped loudly across the empty decks   if you were clairvoyant   dabbled in tarot or worked the Ouija   you might have seen the ghosts begin to dance   too bad: you were too numb one night you found yourself un-alone   talking first cautiously   then wildly   to a man who at first seemed so quiet   parried your conversation   his sentences merging in a synchronicity so startling you let your drink get watery & forgot where you put it   so intoxicated were you both with talk   & the two of you so charmed   laugh now & recall how you thought he said   his name was *Heart* & you   with jitterbug stomach & without smirk   introduced yourself as *Soul*   & each of you unlocked some secret door   walking you along upper decks   he told you sentimental stories of love letters of his grandmother's he'd found in her attic   tied up in ribbons more frail than the pale paper   then he turned the conversation around to bridges   & his hands alive with gestures so grand & sweeping   even he seemed uncertain   about the obscurity of his metaphors   too bad: he seemed a litter's sad-eyed runt   & into the tumbling you gave yourself   O damn that love-drug moonlight: for everything it gives it takes something away   so when he walked you to your cabin & pulled you into his arms   you were a champagne bottle uncorked & poured   as you felt your emotions overflow   & when was it?   just before dawn & dreamy-eyed over cold coffee?   you said you recalled seeing a ghost   dancing moonlit on the ship's bridge   or had you dreamed you'd fallen overboard & woke up soaking wet?   too bad: so were your cheeks   below those sunglasses   leaning against brass deck rails   you could see islands: a green line the trees a white line the beach   moving closer   each one just as isolated   as the broken shells Poseidon settles on the ocean floor   & what are islands anyway?   dead coral & cast-off lava?   bars of sand where palms set down roots?   the dead are still alive   & will start new lives back north where you'll return   when the cruise ship's tugged & docked   so drink the sweet last of island rum from your cup   close your eyes & listen   to the boat's wake spreading behind like a simple truss if you let yourself dream   you'll hear the ghosts start singing   first the chorus   then the bridge

satyr rock [bootleg]

I'm the rock in Virginia Woolf's pocket   I crack open the sky   reflected on the water's mirror   your
gravity of doubt & insecurity   sleeps heavy in the hammock of my coat   in the ink dark room
back home   the clacking iron radiator's rising heat steams the windows   night mist dances &
dervishes over River Ouse & its tributaries & bridges   currents Siren-sing water & force &
pulse & flow & depth   listen: grief is my god   without is my worth   & what I'm not is an electric
spark of ignition   or the throttle rev of a chrome engine Victory motorcycle   or its rider with
his old goat calves   his leather boots & helmet & gloves   fists as if rocks on handlebars   the sudden
roar & whine & scream   drowning out Eurydice shouting out *Orpheus*   I'm the leaving   the
left behind   the wish-girl gone   the highway empty   & as silent as intervals between sinking stones

Orpheus: photo booth [fantasy]

I'm a secret goldfish in an eyeball bowl   a glass cask   a crystal ball   a recording studio sound booth
it's mineshaft quiet   my mic is off a headset talons my ears   I'm a musical mime wearing a
shoulder-strapped guitar   umbilically chorded to the amp stack   toe-tapping foot pedals & distortion
& loops & wah-wah   I'm lip-synch   for my song's my sound my sense of myself   & it's as
if I'm swimming below the surface   deep-diving some obscure wrecked underwaterworld   my hand
reaches out for my muse   to lead me to the next verse   I feel glass scale fish tails   not a school
of fingers   & so   arms extended   my hand-backs rub knuckles   as I kick & scissor & pull   this
gig bag of a body   across riptide & tide & tide pool of white ocean   & so sundered   my eyes
open to meet Echo's eyes looking back: this track is a take   a keeper   the A-side   & it'll go gold

III

underworld

I felt this desire to sing about death
and to praise the deep pools and shoreline
of the fallen landscape that held me.

~ Joseph Millar, "Spanish Blues"

Oh, in the end there is a price exacted
For a young man's joy, for spring and wine.

~ Czeslaw Milosz, *A Treatise on Poetry*

Robert Miltner

blue islands

I

suppose a ship is a stone   skipping wave to whitecap to wish   then imagine an archipelago of whole notes   played by music box ocean   where beach sand and surf offer an homage to home   say sorrow is a seafarer & loss is a longboat   rowing for leagues   over lamentations of waves cresting & crushing troughs   as if branches   bending & breaking   into the distant sea spray

II

as terns & mews float or fly   each manifests a binary of what lasts & what doesn't   as in: gravity is grace   as in: duet is *do not*   the eye of a gull in flight   reveals a story of the earth: each island's a hive & skep   a terrapin & whale spout brooch & bracelet   a shoreline wedding sand to saltwater

III

listen as the blues harmonica becomes a glass harmonium   hear the wave wash ashore   as it pulls & rasps & lapidaries the shoreline   call it a rock ballad of return   a ghost boat discovered docked in Samothrace harbor   call it   a pier dreaming itself a bridge   call it   a chanson for second chances

Orpheus: a ruin of willows

spring arrives & resilient sap is climbing   birches reach as if hands grasping   a wind trembles a willow's guitar string yellow foliage   & look: a knot where a branch was unclasped from hardwood trunk hollowed & burrowed by insects by hive of drones & by pollen-legged honeybees wax-capping combs   by a hard-beaked bird   making a cavity nest   as if a cave-mouth moaning & look closer: embedded inside a bark basket   is the black sun at the center of a tree ring   listen now as I whisper: *Eurydice*   the labyrinth wanderer & the empty birdcage   is sore missed I absent myself & hide in midnight marsh & glade & fen & meadow   how else   except in lightlessness   can I sense her presence?   I shout poems to fallen timbers   call out dire elegies to elm & sumac & black locust   which listen only to Aeolus   hear me you roots where rabbits warren: how can I be you who reach down to pull her up?   listen you slabs & boulders & igneous rocks   you who balance the ball of a stick man's incantation: it is to you I sing these busted ballad verses   this forsaken chorus cracked as if faulted crystal   O you dark stones: plead for me   be interlocutor to deaf mountain Zeus   be fissured granite where my woe drizzles & rains & glazes & freezes & splinters & moves you   as if storm-sundered doors   open your eyes: see ice melt running black   as if from paint brushes   inking lost Eurydice's face   O you marble blocks you hardened magma: you hold secrets & trapped human forms   aching to be hammered free

black nasturtium

Orpheus calls out to Eurydice   but his mouth fills with ants & ash   but his tongue is dust & webs
but her name grows cold in his ear   Eurydice had been as if ripe apricots   golding a laden tree
in an orchard common with apples   had been forget-me-not gone wild in the compost loam
Orpheus feels disrobed   robbed as a robin when winter is coming in   as if an uninvited roisterer
robust & blustery   Orpheus misses how her breath feels   breezing the frets of his neckback   he
laments the loss of her fingers   harp-playing his upright bass of a body   a scarf woven from
torn memories   weights his shoulders   tightens like fists of plum bough & primrose   poppy &
phlox   night's a bed overgrown in love-lies-bleeding   a raft adrift in nightshade   as fireflies
rise as if deranged stars   fallen sycamore leaves   scratch across gravel paths   & the wind papercombs
a window's worn wooden frame   Orpheus listens: not overture   not interlude   not verse   not
refrain   not chorus   not coda   but a dove mourning   but a monotone cello solo   but a lone oboe

autumn peninsula

one blue boat   three triangulated islands   & cliffed passages between   the desire to sail is an aquatic equation awaiting solution   each island is its own encapsulation   both boundary & beginning an evolved identity   that is its own world   though landing offers stillness & stability & structure   I point the bow to the dividing spaces   & row hard toward interstices   where my wonder uncertain in the mist   suspends among fog-cloaked coasts   schooled fish ripple a salt sea surface from seaweed-wrapped rocks   sloe-eyed seals sing as if melancholy Sirens   a solitary eagle screeches & calls its lament for the loss of autumn   as if a prologue to winter   tonight a cup of wine will journey out from my hand to harbor at my mouth   a rocking craft anchored without a pier

Narcissus: the day I drowned

three canoed leaves   lemon yellow or lime green or orange peel   floating in a blue sky river over
its indigo depths   I leaned over the bank   I could not see myself   I was no face in a glass
I was a person displaced   disjoined   dislocated   I was a jettisoned & cast-off mortal   a fractured
manikin   as the deep pool turned into a dark hole   or a lost-track-of mineshaft   an abandoned
well covered in broken branches   or a gilt-framed smoked-glass window   I was an unready fledgling
that felt a plummeting   a falling   a failing instant   as feather turned creek rock   turned stone
turned boulder   I shattered that riffling river   entering where crayfish & catfish & bullfrog & gar
became cold & alabastered gods   & in my ear the water insinuated: *open your mouth   swallow your
life*   & my lungs said: *no*   said: *air*   said: *rise*   & so I arose   exhaling back into light & sound &
known element   my arms grasping   root or branch or crow's wing or the sun itself   but gravity
loved me & pulled me back by foot & leg   hip & waist   torso & arm   neck & mouth   down &
deeper through the cracking sky   into mirrored sloe-black water   silt   eclipsed moon   silence

Echo to Narcissus [dream missive]

wasted time spent building barriers   rock walls   bricks by bric-a-brac   honing my restrained
obsession with doors: oaken slabs & heavy stone   flimsy hollow-outs trimmed in thin veneer
scraped & re-stained & realigned   screens letting heat out & air in   I was both threshold & the rug
shoes slept on just inside the room   until you dear key   latch of my lack   bolt of alacrity
opened me   so that everything hinged on you   only two days ago rain hammered roof & dormer
last night snow swirled & swayed   as if drunken on the moment & deranged   I longed to open
my doors   so as to be your daylily & damselfly   for missing you forced a closure of my eyes   I felt
my mouth open as would a window   feel the breeze pass through portals   heard curtains
moving as if shadows of lost birds   imagined a box of light falling   through casement & illuminating
the floor I stood upon   in a room made of screen & glass   with my ear placed   to that empty
space   where love happened   my sweet pane & I listened to you speak   but my body spoke for I
could not   & it became agent for ink & cut feather   as if chorus following verse   our shadows
arrived as the door closed over the threshold   frame & lintel   liminal hallway & water-wrapped pier
dune & shore   a lake where two birds cross the mirror   in which you too much loved yourself

sugar & salt

Eurydice's lips were cane sugar   what a sweet tooth she gave Orpheus   for mouth is tongue is lick
is love is pillow talk honeyed into a lover's ear   how her scent remains: cardamom & cocoa
coca & cinnamon   now he's the gourmet of her ghost   her descent tore love's blanket into separate
sheets   as if pages of inscribed lyrics   fallen from his notebook   & as he steps from an ocean
swim   the sea drops shaken from his beard   ink the beach   & create a pattern resembling Eurydice's
features   yet under sunlight her face dissipates   Orpheus turns to the beach behind him: no
one is there   only waves cresting white tridents   & so up a mountain trail   to the highest point of
Samothrace their secret aerie he climbs   again he looks behind: yet Eurydice is not there
Orpheus muses: *if the fire of love requited gifts wings   & lifts lovers into the sky*   Orpheus wonders: *why then
such a damning fall   though rock & salt & sand & orchard & island & ocean into the underearth?*   Orpheus
hears a waxwing   hears the laughter of three ageless gossips   Orpheus looks back: a pillar of sea salt

the river Nox & the caves of Hypnos [fantasy]

Orpheus exhales   & sets down the hash pipe   smoke ribbons & disappears   a dusky sleep god
murmurs & invokes & induces drowsiness   it whispers: *memory's other name is ghost*   it insinuates:
a ghost's other name is Eurydice   a box crafted of cedar & cypress & juniper   latch clacked &
uncloistered & lifted   Orpheus arrays seashells & teacups & halved walnuts   each apertures
secrets: a satyr's laughter   a blue guitar   scent of poppy   & taste of forget-me-not leaves   steeped
in water drawn from a river   whose name's a nest of spiders & sparrows dumb under his tongue

alackaday the wintery orchard

heavy the slumbering of the bee hive   silent & still the cider press   the dismay of apple boughs
unbudded   in the absence of spring's soft crescendo   of blossoms & colorful universes of
fruited planets   in the paper-comb row of scarecrow trees   snow swirls & whorls & swarms both
field & pasture   look: blank sheets of linen   charcoaled with stick figure branches   where
snow is dance & wind is song   November: bleached ghost globes   December: brisk gusts whirl &
dismiss dreams of robin revivals   a cardinal pecks blanched crab apples   the delicious arrival
of desire: bee to bud to flower to fruit to basket to market   Apollo recalls brusque color   & Calliope
remembers the sun's taste on a tongue   each spring dressed in vestal white   she relives wedding's
velocity   Calliope tells Orpheus: *your father pushed me on a swing in an apple tree & I flew like a red bird*
each autumn Apollo falls   as if deception's russet messenger   as sleet dispatches birds' tracks
& ice quiets wind's lyre   winter erases its missives   laughs Aeolus   & summer's a lost love letter

scatter my heart you three-sistered muse

a waning moon has fallen behind the fencepost & birches   a bafflement of fireflies   pulses & multiplies in mulberry trees   the apple grove's a charm   as was our cunningly-made island the dream of Eurydice   seems now a counterfeit creation   devised of things gleaned from the unseen & felt as excitement as excess as ecstasy   love is a treasure-trove   no one has hands enough to hold   what poor heretics were we   duped & believing   we'd constructed a radical constancy denying a sun's but a season & the moon's a moment   & what breaks with a day may be sere & sorrowful   & now an unruly sun calls as if to cauterize our loss   look: an eclipse of chimney swifts   is swept from the sky   bats perform acrobatic arcs   ink overwrites the crescent moon with night's erasure   two kinds of incongruent fool were we: one for the choric echo of waves on Samothrace Island   & one for illusionary roads to candled rooms   where old radios played tin pan alley cat love songs long into night   so ghosts can dance & never die   listen you three old women   you crones & grackles   I invoke you: overthrow & forge me anew   let her fractured wax wings be my raiment   & her lost breath fill the fractures & interstices   that ache my lyric lines

Morpheus: changeling in the looking-glass

O troubadour & elegist   catch my scent   I'm the wild onion hard in the palm   as if acorn or walnut
or rock   & as soft to the mouth as cool water   hand-cupped from a spring   O Orpheus
you lamp pull   balled paper   bell gripped by the clapper   apple held by dried stem   can't you see
I'm your mute mirrored twin   hanging by an umbilical cord   unable to tell   how many skin-
layers you'll need to peel back   before we find & face each other?   listen runaway brother: a mystery's
a wren's nest held under our tongues   & revealed as layers unriddle   a miracle's what happens
as grape vines are reset in better *terroir*   stretching toward silver suns   too long you've been held
tight as autumn bulbs   or summer's skeletal strung cayenne   O Orpheus   be neither dried
herb stored in a bottle and tossed into the sea   nor be sad brother to nutmeg & peppercorn & ginger
root   O Orpheus   be loss's fracturing secret   you whisper   into tree cavity & seashell &
wine cup & guitar sound hole & cave opening   O be the impossible singer of summer's sudden fall

mockingbird [blues jam]

against an opaque windowpane   rain thrums a chilling rhythm for unsleeping Orpheus   an eclipsed
moon is a mute black hole returning his stare   he aches from lack & loss   as he runs hands
through hair   at his fingertips the notebook is a locked door   each page shuttered   against an inked
feather   to loosen his thoughts   a guitar expresses what envious tongues cannot speak   & is
as dangerous as chisel or chalk or stick or sword or word   as if the way an artist's brush   applies
gesso & paint to a canvas   as if silence is preparation for music making   holding the guitar in
his hands is as if mimetic courtship   lyre-like to find solace   palms enjoined with Eurydice   &
clenching his fist   a sleight of hand forms forefinger & index & ring finger   into a minor chord
O how he feels a need to play the muses' three chord rock   picture his electric guitar as if a body
see its strings as if veins & arteries   feel a fretted neck as if spine   watch how fingers move
across the guitar   hand as if a long-leg spider   spinning filament & silk along the frets & adding
henna design to the pearl inlay   each waiting note joins in waking melody as musician &
instrument duel   in improvisation's riff & jam delirium   as if furies enter the body through a tarantula
bite   hear how the tempo grows in increasing rapidity   & erratic frenzied snapping of fingers
as if an ecstatic magical ritual in a temple to Dionysus   look at unrecognizable Orpheus playing
closed-eyed his Stratocaster as he trance-tap dances   gyrations & gesticulations & convulsions
& electric shock shakes: this is hypnotic exorcism as curative   this is dervished leap & scream of
revival & revision   this is a dog that eats the gods for transmigration of souls   this is Aeolus
charming & chiming the wind   this is Apollo striking flint to ignite spark to fire to voice to poetry
this is the ghost of Eurydice   & this is insomniac Orpheus   playing the *don't you look back* blues

Orpheus in Vegas [dream song]

he turned to look back: a chorus of neon tourists tumbling from cabs & limos   from casinos pulsing
poppy music   his hands hung as if busted drums   & his voice entranced: vocal chords taut
tongue become stone   mouth a mute lyre   a scarecrow's ragged songs   & a glimpse of the green-
eyed muse   eluding & fading   how his ears ached   for the sound of leaves at sunrise   seen
from the island highpoint of Samothrace   or gusting sunset cool along shore   a duet of waves
crashing cymbals   timpani & aftermath   & the arrival of Echo   then he felt a beat in his
bones   rhythm in his wrists   he played walls like bodhráns   power lines grabbed & strummed
became banjos   stomped streets transformed to steel drums   traffic stopped to listen   & then
he sang: it was as if he was Aeolus   calling winds from the farthest of the west   he played his body
harp   scales in major keys praising his muse   & minor keys keening her loss   in an underground
barking dog parking garage on the Strip   somewhere between *Mandalay Bay & The Rio*   O wonder!
Orpheus sang   O wonder! Echo refrained & looked back: three salt pillars crumbling   O wonder!
green-eyed Eurydice enjoined   embracing wide-eyed Orpheus   & handing him his re-strung guitar

Orpheus: once a traveler

the boatman rows me   from sea harbor to a blue island   circular as a brass bowl   heavy rain is as
if a waterfall   I stay on the glazed craft   & look across oarlocks at rocks   standing longer
than music or muse   torn apart by wind   & eroded by centuries of storms   loud thunderclouds
move   across a dark gray sky   as if centaurs in sooted snow: answer   reverberate   & echo
under a plum wine dark silk sky   the ocean seems as if pressed   from the skins of grapes   so I make
ink   & from a blue heron feather   I cut a pen   so as to tattoo words   in orchard rows of
poetry   petitioning for the longevity   of inscribed memory   my recollection is a crane's eye   so I
recite poems   expressing three true things: how trust is a tree   balanced on a mountain
precipice where waters fall   & how love is bee skep is cup is terrapin is island   rocked in the shawled
arms of waves   & how autumn must close like chrysanthemums   so spring can open its irises

Echo: coda & envoi [found song]

my song of loss   transects the horizon in constant quest of luster   as in a sepia photo   silken threads of falling water   under canopy & branch   clamoring to be poems   as if tattoos written on cotton paper   among whitecaps & cumulus clouds in a room of white ocean   *adieu* to the obscure light stopping at unintended intervals culled from catacombs   seen as if shadow & shawl crazy as a grounded bird   as a gypsy tambourine   as brush strokes of cirrus clouds   frosted are the dormers coming over the top of the wall   as if an arrow notching its bowstring in the gentle breeze   so enchanted audiences could strut arcing toward the runway's end   denounced in a dunce cap   from island to archipelago   through the power of magnification seeing below only mystery & immortality of the island rum reflected on the water's mirror across riptide & tide & tide pool into the distant sea spray   cracked as if faulted crystal   overgrown in love-lies-bleeding from seaweed-wrapped rocks exhaling back into light & sound   where two birds cross the mirror as if pages of inscribed lyrics clacked & uncloistered   as sleet dispatches birds' tracks denying a sun's but a season held under our tongues in improvisation's riff & jam delirium   & a scarecrow's ragged song in orchard rows of poetry: echo

Notes

"apple trees in bloom" is in response to the painting *Apple Tree in Bloom* by Gustave Caillebotte

"Eurydice: symphony in green & gold" is in response to the painting *Symphony in Green and Gold* by Thomas Wilmer Dewing

"water lilies" is written in response to the painting *Lotus Lilies* by Charles Courtney Curran

"alchemy calling" is in response to the painting *Gray and Gold* by John Rodgers Cox

"Eurydice waiting" is in response to the painting *Black and Gold* by Thomas Wilmer Dewing

"three gossips: ballad for a blue guitar" was inspired by the "Chagall and the Russian Avant-Garde" exhibition at the Art Gallery of Toronto

"summer's ending [song]" is in response to the painting *Summer's Ending* by Jared French

"snow at Louveciennes & rain in Arles [song]" is in response to the painting *Snow at Louveciennes* by Alfred Sisley

"Cupid & Psyche [song]" is in response to the painting *Cupid and Psyche* by Jacques-Louis David

"the green door [song]" is written in response to the painting *In the Doorway (Good Morning)* by Frederick Carl Frieseke

"painting the town wine [cover song]" was inspired by the song "Coquette" by Gus Kahn, John W. Green, and Carmen Lombardo

"clatter of jackdaws: Eurydice as a sorry sight [alternate take]" was inspired by the nursery rhyme "One for Sorrow"

"portrait of Echo as Camille Monet in a red cape [song]" is in response to *The Red Kerchief* by Claude Monet

"lost at sea: Hart's song" is for poet Hart Crane. His mother's name was Grace. His father, Clarence, invented Life Saver candy. A commemorative marker in Garrettsville, Ohio states that Crane was "lost at sea"

"autumn peninsula" is in response to a kimono painting by Itchiku Kubota

"scatter my heart you three-sistered muse" was inspired by the poem "Batter My Heart, Three-personed God" by John Donne

"Morpheus: changeling in the looking-glass" is for Robert Bly

"Orpheus: once a traveler" was written in response to the scrolls *Four of Eight Views of the Xiao and Xiang Rivers* by Tani Bunchō

Acknowledgments

Peter Grandbois

California Review: "Rain"

Chariton Review: "The way sky moves"

Chiron Review: "Sometimes I'm not sure what memory is worth," "The bridge," and "The veil between worlds is thin"

Crack the Spine: "There is no one to write this"

decomP: "[Hollowness seeps in when I wake]"

Denver Quarterly: "[Why not this other dream]"

Diode: "Something like faith"

Event: "Now begins the silent season" and "That we do not perish"

Fifth Wednesday: "The breaking of tongues"

Flights: "[All we know of stone]," "[The alchemist is thinking of his secrets]," and "[The universe is like a corpse]"

The Gettysburg Review: "[Sometimes I think I hear]"

Glassworks: "A prayer to fall like dust in search of a home" and "The color of hands"

Healing Muse: "Waiting for revelation" and "So close to steam over a river"

The Inflectionist Review: "The doctor said he was fine" and "The ballet of the broken"

Juked: "What the night has to say"

Louisiana Literature: "Only in the dark" and "[When the body forgets]"

Main Street Rag: "Someone lit my memory on fire"

Meridian: "As if darkness doesn't come drop by drop"

Midwest Quarterly: "[How am I only]"

Nottingham Review: "The way we push through light"

Red Paint Hill: "To return to things their stillness"

Rust + Moth: "A long way back"

Salamander: "This mad dance"

Solstice: "What mud-drunk song waits"

Southern Indiana Review: "[My body haunts itself]"

UCity Review: "Light water beneath the dark" and "The sacrifice of things hurts at first"

The Worcester Review: "Here is where it ends"

James McCorkle

Barrow Street: sections 8-10 of "Euphrates"
Colorado Review: "In Time" and sections 1-5 of "Euphrates"
Crazyhorse: "Barn Fire," "May Days," "May Suspensions," "Source Code," and "Updraft"
Fiddlehead: "Dog-Fox" and "On Recollection"
Gulfcoast: "February Journal"
Harvard Review: "September Notes"
Kenyon Review: "The Water Column"
Mānoa: "Fox-Sparrow"
New England Review: "Hornets" and "House Crickets"
Phoebe: "Measures"
Red Wheelbarrow: "Azulitos," "Cicada," "Kill Holes," and "The Visible World"
Stone Canoe: "Fusillade" and "Falling Birds"
Web / Conjunctions: "Thule"

Robert Miltner

Angle: Journal of Art and Culture: "Cupid & Psyche [love song]"
Birmingham Poetry Review: "snow at Louveciennes and rain in Arles [song]," "apple trees in bloom," and "water lilies"
Bluestem: "summer's ending [song]"
Buried Letter: "coincidence of direction," "painting the town wine [cover song]," "portrait of Eurydice as theater & thespian," and "the river Nox & the caves of Hypnos [fantasy]"
The Heartlands Today The Mythic Midwest Issue: "lost at sea: Hart's song"
Mixed Fruit: "Eurydice rising"
Pacific Review: A West Coast Arts Review Annual: Errant Mythologies Issue: "studio session [sound check]"
The Rappahannock Review: "Eurydice as a charcoal sketch," "idleness & indolence [love song]," and "shore line: epistle to Eurydice"
Read Water (Locked Horns Press anthology): "Narcissus: the day I drowned"
Queen Mab & the Moon Boy (Kattywompus Press chapbook): "autumn peninsula"
Greatest Hits (Pudding House Press chapbook): "portrait of Echo as Camille Monet in a red cape"
Imperative (All Nations Press chapbook): "alackaday the wintery orchard" and "Morpheus: changeling in the looking-glass"
Ghost of a Chance (Zygote Press/Idlewild Press limited edition chapbook, intaglio prints by Wendy Collin Soren): "Paris: ghost of a chance [unrequited love song]"
Eurydice Rising (Red Berry Editions limited edition chapbook, designed and hand-bound by Marie Dern): "Eurydice rising," "epithalamium [dream song]," "sugar & salt," "black nasturtium," "Orpheus in Vegas [dream song]," "blue islands," and "Orpheus: once a traveler"

Two Trains Too Many (Blue Caboose CD, music composed and performed by Erin Vaughn): "green door [tone poem]"

Three Songs, (recital of music composed by Sebastian Anthony Birch, performed by vocalist Melissa Davis, with piano by Jerry Wong): "summer's ending [song]," "Eurydice: coincidence of remembrance [dream song]," and "portrait of Echo as Camille Monet in a red cape [song]"

Special appreciation for support in the completion of this book from Research and Graduate Studies at Kent State University for a Creative Activity Grant, and from the Ohio Arts Council for an Individual Excellence Award in Poetry

About The Authors

Peter Grandbois is the author of nine previous books, the most recent of which is *Kissing the Lobster* (Spuyten Duyvil, 2018). His poems, stories, and essays have appeared in over one hundred journals. His plays have been performed in St. Louis, Columbus, Los Angeles, and New York. He is a senior editor at *Boulevard* magazine and teaches at Denison University.

James McCorkle is the author of *Evidences* (selected by Jorie Graham for the 2003 *APR*-Honickman First Book Award) and *The Subtle Bodies* (Etruscan Press, 2014). He is a recipient of fellowships from Ingram Merrill and the NEA, he teaches at Hobart and William Smith Colleges.

Robert Miltner's prose poetry collection is *Hotel Utopia* (New Rivers Press, 2011), winner of the Many Voices Project poetry prize; prizes include a Wick Chapbook award, a Red Berry Editions Chapbook Award, and an Ohio Arts Council Award. An emeritus professor at Kent State University Stark, he is on the poetry and fiction faculty of the NEOMFA.

Also by

Peter Grandbois

Fiction:
The Girl on the Swing and At Night in Crumbling Voices
The Glob Who Girdled Granville and The Secret Lives of Actors
Wait Your Turn and The Stability of Large Systems
Domestic Disturbances
Nahoonkara
The Gravedigger

Nonfiction:
Kissing the Lobster
The Arsenic Lobster: A Hybrid Memoir

Poetry:
This House That

James McCorkle

The Subtle Bodies
Evidences
Conversant Essays: Contemporary Poets on Poetry (Editor)
The Still Performance: Writing, Self, and Interconnection in Five Postmodern American Poets

Robert Miltner

Poetry:
Hotel Utopia

Poetry Chapbooks:
Imperative
Queen Mab and the Moon Boy
Fellow Traveler
Rock the Boat

Greatest Hits
Canyons of Sleep
A Box of Light
On the Off-Ramp
Against the Simple
Seamless Serial Hour

Poetry Limited Editions:
Eurydice Rising (Red Berry Editions)
Ghost of a Chance (Zygote/Idlewild Press)

Short Fiction:
And Your Bird Can Sing

Books from Etruscan Press

Etruscan Press Is Proud of Support Received From

Wilkes University

Youngstown State University

The Ohio Arts Council

The Stephen & Jeryl Oristaglio Foundation

The Nathalie & James Andrews Foundation

The National Endowment for the Arts

The New Mexico Community Foundation

Founded in 2001 with a generous grant from the Oristaglio Foundation, Etruscan Press is a nonprofit cooperative of poets and writers working to produce and promote books that nurture the dialogue among genres, achieve a distinctive voice, and reshape the literary and cultural histories of which we are a part.

etruscan press

www.etruscanpress.org

Etruscan Press books may be ordered from

Consortium Book Sales and Distribution

800.283.3572

www.cbsd.com

Etruscan Press is a 501(c)(3) nonprofit organization.
Contributions to Etruscan Press are tax deductible
as allowed under applicable law.
For more information, a prospectus,
or to order one of our titles,
contact us at books@etruscanpress.org.